JOHN NASH
the painter as illustrator

JOHN NASH
the painter as illustrator

JOHN LEWIS

With a Foreword by
Wilfrid Blunt

THE PENDOMER PRESS

Published in Great Britain 1978 by
Potter Books Limited
The Raswell, Loxhill
Godalming, Surrey GU8 4BQ

ISBN 0 906267 00 5

Published in Canada 1978 by
Monk Bretton Books
1 Dale Avenue
Toronto
Ontario M4W 1K2

Printed in Great Britain

Set in 12/15 Monotype Baskerville
and printed letterpress by
The Compton Press Ltd, The Old Brewery, Tisbury, Wilts
offset by
Skelton's Press, Wellingborough, Northants
bound by
Weatherby-Woolnough, Wellingborough

CANADIAN CATALOGUING IN PUBLICATION DATA
Lewis, John, 1912–
JOHN NASH
Bibliography: p.
ISBN 0-920538-00-2
ISBN 0-920538-01-0 (limited ed.)
1. Nash, John Northcote, 1893–1977
2. Painters – England – Biography
3. Illustrators – England – Biography
ND497.N28L49   759.2   C77-001837-8

On the title-page:
SLEEPING CATS wood engraving *c.* 1924

opposite page:
SEA CAMPION pen drawing from the *Aldeburgh Festival Programme Book* 1956

Acknowledgements

To John Nash himself who even in his last illness gave me all the help I could ask for and to Ronald Blythe for help in searching for material at Bottengoms and for advice on my manuscript. I would also like to thank the following who have helped in various ways with their memories of the artist or in their writings about his work: The Earl and Countess of Cranbrook, the late Robert Bevan, Mrs. Natalie Bevan, Anthony d'Offay, Mrs. Anstice Shaw, Frederick Gore, R.A., John Sanson and Sir John Rothenstein.

I am grateful to the Trustees of the John Nash estate for permission to reproduce most of the illustrations in the book. Finally my gratitude to my wife Griselda for her help in both design and production.

Contents

List of illustrations

Colour Plates

opposite page :
HORNED POPPY pen drawing from the *Aldeburgh Festival Programme Book* 1956

Foreword
by
Wilfrid Blunt

If John Nash had never painted a picture or made a single drawing in his life, I think he would still deserve to be remembered for his kindness, his generosity and his personal charm. He had what is today called (by those who have no idea what the word really means) 'charisma'; he had it also in its true sense of 'divinely conferred talent'. I met him, alas, only two or three times, but that was enough: enough, I mean of course, to appreciate what a rare person he was.

On the first occasion I called on him, uninvited and unheralded, because, chancing to find myself within striking distance of his improbably named and remote house, Bottengoms, I felt the urge to seize the opportunity to meet him and tell him how much I admired his flower drawings. He immediately made me welcome, produced a portfolio of his work and said, 'Choose a drawing – whichever one you like.' I chose an exquisite but rather slight pencil sketch of *Geranium armenum*. 'Oh no!' he cried, 'take a better one than that!' But I refused; of its kind it was perfect, and how could I, a complete stranger, accept an important, more valuable drawing?

Now I have more than once been summoned by my bank manager to his office; but never once has he led me to his strongroom and said, 'Here are some of my banknotes; do choose any one you like.' Nor can I imagine that, had I chosen a pound note, he would have begged me to prefer one of a higher denomination. Usually he suggested that some reduction of my overdraft would not be unacceptable.

But all this has nothing to do with John Nash the illustrator – and looking at the plates in John Lewis's timely and attractive book I realised how much wider was the artist's range than I had known before. For example, there is his delightful and highly personal sense of humour; the suspense as one waits for that fly on the head of the aged club bore to be swatted (p. 54) is almost unbearable. I may be prejudiced, but I believe, however, that it is as a botanical illustrator that John Nash will principally come to be remembered. Like Hans Weiditz, who four centuries earlier designed the triumphant woodcuts for Brunfels' *Herbarum Vivae Eicones*, he gives us the portrait of a particular flower. He draws not *a* geranium but *that particular geranium*. Look, for example, at the two sunflower heads on p. 100: you would pick them out at once in an identity parade with a thousand sunflowers lined up for inspection.

The reason why he wanted to do this was because he passionately loved the individual flower; he succeeded in doing it because he had such a marvellous eye and such miraculous sureness of touch. I like best of all his swift pencil and his pen drawings; occasionally the wood engravings are, in my humble opinion, a shade stodgy; and in this medium, as in lithography, there are other illustrators among his contemporaries who are his equal.

Two years ago, when Anthony d'Offay staged an exhibition of John Nash's wood-engravings, illustrations and drawings of plants, the artist was persuaded to write a short autobiographical essay, *The Artist Plantsman*. In it he told that for nearly seventy years he had drawn plants for love or of necessity, adding, 'I feel a slight pencil flourish even of a part of a plant is more valuable than a photograph.' Who, looking at his work, could fail to agree?

WILFRID BLUNT
The Watts Gallery, Compton

opposite page : THE WHEAT HARVEST pen drawing from *Rural Rides* 1930
By permission of Peter Davies Ltd

JOHN NASH
the painter as illustrator

JOHN NASH drawing by Powys Evans 1931

opposite page :
SEA PEA pen drawing used on the cover of the *Aldeburgh Festival Programme Book* 1956

I

'A man of letters'

It is an extraordinary fact that no book has been written about John Nash, an English landscape painter of unique importance and a botanical draughtsman of genius. His worth was recognised by his fellow Academicians when in 1967 he was the first living artist to be honoured with a Retrospective Exhibition in the main galleries of Burlington House. Other honours came his way. In 1964 he was made a Commander of the British Empire and also an Honorary Fellow of the Royal College of Art; in 1967 Essex University gave him an Honorary Degree. As for publications about his work, there is a booklet published by *The Fleuron* in 1927, there is a perceptive essay by Sir John Rothenstein in *Modern English Painters* and there are articles on his work in various magazines, but there is no book.

Rothenstein's opinion was that John Nash was 'so dedicated and so reticent'. He went on to explain this by saying:

'The landscapes of John Nash are uncommon in that they are the work of a countryman. His brother Paul also loved landscape but he brought to his interpretations of it a town-sharpened and innately literary intelligence and town-forged weapons, but John is a country-man by lifelong residence and in all his interests. Where Paul would write a manifesto or form a group, John transplants some roses; where Paul would cherish the words of Sir Thomas Browne or Blake, John consults a seed catalogue.'

The pleasure of looking at John Nash's illustrations and engravings is greatly enhanced if one knows something of the man himself and his mainstream work. The bare facts of John Nash's early career can be set down very briefly.

John Northcote Nash was the second son of William Harry Nash, barrister-at-law and Recorder of Abingdon. He was born in Kensington on 11 April 1893, where he lived until 1901 when his family, which included his brother Paul and his sister Barbara, moved to Buckinghamshire. He was educated, first at Langley Place, Slough, and then at Wellington College. For a few months after leaving school he worked as an unpaid journalist on the *Middlesex and Berks Gazette* before starting work as a painter and comic draughtsman.

In 1913 John Nash and his elder brother Paul had a joint exhibition at a gallery in South Kensington. The success of this exhibition proved the wisdom of his choice of career and, as a result of the approval bestowed on his work by the Fitzroy Street painters and particularly by Harold Gilman, he was elected in 1914 to the newly formed London Group.

In 1916 John Nash joined up and was posted to the Artists' Rifles and served with them on the Western Front until January 1918. The horrors of those days were mitigated for him by letters full of joy and fun from Dora Carrington. In a letter written early in the war Carrington mentions 'an interesting girl who wears glasses' who was at the Slade with her. This was Christine Kuhlenthal, later to become his wife.

In 1918 John Nash was commissioned as an official war artist and in the same year he married. The Nashes lived at Gerrards Cross until 1921, in which year he was elected a member of the New English Art Club. In the following year they moved to a cottage near Prince's Risborough at the foot of the Chilterns, where he began to develop his interest in gardening and in plant drawing.

In the early years of their married life they were very poor. Christine's father was always urging his son-in-law to take up 'commercial art' or to do something useful. Christine, however, was a wonderful manager. She darned and patched their clothes and concocted meals out of practically nothing. She earned a little money by dressmaking and by teaching dancing. John Nash meanwhile continued with complete single-mindedness to draw and paint, though on one or two occasions when they had barely sixpence in the house, they took the produce of their garden to the local market.

Throughout their marriage his wife's unselfishness and constant cheerfulness gave John Nash a setting in which he could devote all his energies to his own affairs.

In 1924 he was given his first teaching job. This was at the Ruskin School of Drawing in Oxford where he taught until 1929. During this time he started work on *Poisonous Plants*, his first important commission.

After leaving the Ruskin School John Nash rented first of all a little bungalow alongside Wormingford Mill. When that was burned down he took a cottage near Bures. There he began to paint the East Anglian landscape. These paintings were exhibited in 1930 at his one-man show at the Goupil Gallery. All his painting expeditions were preceded by Christine doing a reconnaissance of suitable painting sites.

In 1934 he joined the staff of the Royal College of Art as an assistant Teacher of Design; this was during Sir William Rothenstein's last year as Principal.

★   ★   ★   ★   ★

I first met John Nash at Tunbridge Wells in the summer of 1941. I was running an Army Camouflage School for South-Eastern Command and had had a request to lay on a camouflage course for the Navy. In addition to twenty or so naval officers, there were two officers from the Royal Marines. They were respectively Major Alan Durst and Captain John Nash. One evening during the course they came up to our flat in Mount Sion.

John Nash was then forty-eight years old, a slightly built figure, auburn-haired though balding, with a tanned complexion and heavy lidded eyes. I ingenuously showed him some drawings of boats that I had done. His interest in them was no more than polite, but when my wife Griselda rather reluctantly produced some of her flower drawings, his interest was immediately aroused. This interest in plants became a lasting bond between them.

As the evening drew on, the impression I had formed of him on the course deepened. It was of his quiet charm, his warmth and his modesty. He had the air of an old-fashioned English gentleman, tempered with a certain earthiness. Alan Durst, who was a sculptor and John Nash's senior both in age and rank, seemed to think the world of him. It is difficult to convey such an indefinite attribute as charm. Charm he certainly had and in such good measure that many women loved him and men went out of their way to do things for him.

The next time I saw John Nash was in the February after the war. By

BRITANNIA IN WINTER QUARTERS watercolour 1939

that time he had moved to Bottengoms Farmhouse at Wormingford in Essex. I had found a job with Cowells, a firm of printers in Ipswich, and was staying in rooms until I could find a house. I knew no one in Ipswich, but I had John Nash's telephone number. I telephoned him and he invited me to lunch on the following Sunday. I had no car, so he said that either he or his wife would meet me at Colchester Station.

By the weekend there had been a heavy fall of snow and it was Christine Nash who met me at Colchester. She was then in her early fifties. During the drive we talked. I found her observations about people we both knew shrewd, witty, even tart. She was rather reserved, yet there was a warmth in her manner. At times she looked a little sad. What I did not know then was they had lost their only son at the age of five in a motor car accident. This tragedy had left its mark on both of them. They rarely referred to the child.

At Wormingford, the snow was lying thickly in the fields. The driftway to Bottengoms farmhouse is a deep, sunk track leading down into the valley, nearly half a mile long. On that Sunday it was blocked by snow five feet deep, so we had to leave the car and walk.

18

BRISTOL DOCKS line and watercolour drawing from *A Handbook of Printing Types* 1947

Conditions at Bottengoms were primitive. There was no electricity and the source of water was from a stream that ran in an open culvert across the kitchen floor, which made the kitchen somewhat colder than the garden outside. They had no need of refrigerators, for near the kitchen door was a little waterfall which served as a place to keep the butter and milk cool in very hot weather.

John and Christine lived happily, each in their own way, in this remote spot for the rest of their married life. Slowly, as they became better off, they made it more comfortable, which included diverting the stream.

Within a few years John created the most beautiful garden, filled with rare and unusual plants. The garden lay in a steep-sided valley. There were various ponds around which grew all kinds of willow, including *Salix tortuosa* whose twisted branches, twigs and leaves looked as if the tree had been struck by lightning. At the head of the top pond *Petasites japonicus* and *Gunnera manicata*, looking like giant rhubarb with its six-foot stems and yard-wide leaves, added an even more exotic note to the surroundings.

The approach to the house was through an orchard that he had planted with quince, greengages and plums. Behind the orchard, and in great contrast to the romantic layout of the rest of the garden, was an immaculate kitchen plot with ordered rows of vegetables and fruit divided by wide grass paths.

Along the flagged path near the house were old stone sinks filled with succulents and alpine plants and there were always lots of old-fashioned pinks including a pretty prim one with white flowers blotched with pink markings called *Painted Lady*, and another called *Dad's Favourite*. John Nash delighted in the names of plants, one in particular that he used to utter with relish was *Cappadocian Venus's Navelwort*, which had little bright blue flowers. Near the kitchen door, which also served as the front door, stood a big, old spreading Blenheim Orange. Beyond this there was a gate leading to a tumbledown barn set in a tangled thicket of willows. This barn often appeared in his paintings, for his studio window looked down onto it.

In front of the house old-fashioned roses grew in profusion, pink-striped *Rosa mundi*, delicate shell-pink *Madame Pierre Oger* and dark crimson *Cardinal Richelieu*.

The house itself was a typical little sixteenth- or seventeenth-century East Anglian farmhouse, frame built and plastered, though the south gable-end was of brick, and covered with a prolific vine. Inside there were no passages, low ceilinged room opening into low ceilinged room. The sitting-room was dominated by a Steinway grand piano on which John and Christine used to play duets – Bach, Mozart and Schubert

THE TORTOISE pen drawing from *A Handbook of Printing Types* 1947

being their favourite composers. This piano had been left to Christine by her father, and in his will he had given instructions that Steinways should tune and service the piano throughout his daughter's life. Above the piano hung a landscape of the Gloucestershire countryside that John Nash had painted in 1915. There was also another early painting by him of a village near Florence. In addition to these there were paintings given to him by his artist friends, by Eric and Tirzah Ravilious, by Lett Haines, and Peter Coker. There were also some flowers which Ronald Blythe had picked on Paul's grave and had had framed.

In the winter time the sitting-room was heated by a rather meagre little fire in a hob grate. The mantelpiece was always thick with gallery cards and there were one or two Staffordshire figures including one of Jenny Lind. There was a chaise longue under the south window on which Christine used to curl up with one or other of her cats. The rest of the wall space was taken up with books, particularly books about flowers and gardening and fishing. There was practically nothing about art and artists, but there were Everyman editions of Richardson, Smollett and Jane Austen. In 1977, after Christine's death, John and Ronald Blythe together read all of Jane Austen's novels. John Nash's other reading consisted of lives of generals from Wellington to Montgomery and, with Christine, he shared a taste for 'whodunits' – anything from Raymond Chandler to Dick Francis. There were two books quite apart from all these that meant more to him than all the others. The first was Gilbert White's *The Natural History of Selborne* and the second was George Borrow's *The Bible in Spain*, the only book he took to the First World War. On his father's advice he always carried it in his breast pocket as a possible protection against a stray spent bullet.

In the dimly lit kitchen at Bottengoms there were two of his brother Paul's paintings and a corner cupboard filled with a pretty Coalport tea service. Alongside the kitchen range was an almost vertical cupboard staircase leading up to the bedrooms, again one opening into another, and finally into John's studio, a small, dark L-shaped room. That he painted quite large pictures in this dark little attic shows how oblivious he must have been to such difficulties. This room, which he always kept neat and tidy, was the antithesis of what the layman might imagine a painter's studio to be like. It was at one with the artist, devoid of pretension.

Over the next few years we saw much of John and Christine. In June we used to meet at Aldeburgh. The first Aldeburgh Festival took place in 1948 under the inspired guidance of Benjamin Britten and Peter Pears and at it there was an exhibition of contemporary paintings by East Anglian artists. The small selection committee included John Nash and among the artists contributing was his old friend Claughton

IRONBRIDGE watercolour drawing 1956

Pellew. In 1956 the ninth Aldeburgh Festival programme book was illustrated by John Nash with pen drawings of local places and flowers. He drew that celebrated Aldeburgh plant *Lathyrus maritimus,* or Sea Pea for the cover.

Soon after I had arrived at Cowells, Geoffrey Smith, one of their two managing directors, asked me if I would produce a type specimen book for them. I knew little about type so I filled the book with illustrations by all the contemporary artists I could think of, including of course John Nash. The drawings that John Nash did for that modest book were the first of several projects that we worked on together over the years.

One of the drawings for the Cowells book was to illustrate an extract from Ruskin's *The Harbours of England,* for which he drew a picture of the Bristol docks with one of his beloved paddle steamers towing a sailing ship. This drawing was based on sketches he had made when visiting Bristol before the war.

Among other jobs on which we worked were a book on English flowers for Mervyn Horder at Duckworths, a calendar for Cowells, an

23

advertisement drawing for Crittalls, illustrations and a cover for a Shell Chemical agricultural magazine, two illustrated editions of Gilbert White's *The Natural History of Selborne*, a set of amusing illustrations for an anthology of Suffolk verse edited by Lord Cranbrook and illustrations for a book on fishing for Evans Brothers.

John was a good person to work with even if whilst he was doing the job there would be a few piteous moans about the difficulties of bad light or about the weather or how green the landscape was. He developed a positive phobia about green and it frequently crops up in the letters he used to write to us on his annual painting holidays. Paul Nash's observation[1] about his brother's intention to become a 'man of letters' was literally fulfilled over the years, for whenever he was weather-bound on holiday, he would sit down and write to all his 'dear ones' as he called his friends.

Although most of his letters were written on holiday, one came to us from Wormingford dated 1 January 1950 after he had been laid up for Christmas with influenza:

'. . . the germs fled before the combined attack of penicillin and M & B leaving me as if several steam rollers had been over the old corpse and a feeling that I hardly cared if one or two more rolled over – and when I say steam rollers, I mean the real old-fashioned kind, complete with funnel and a prancing horse device on the breast plate – not those wretched little modern affairs that are coming into fashion with county councils today.'

The little detail about the steam roller is typical of his wry and personal kind of observation.

Most of his letters to my wife have some reference to flora. In 1950 he wrote to Griselda from Penrhyndeudraeth, near Snowdon:

'The Welsh do not appear to go in for gardening and there's hardly a flower in any cottage garden far less any choice subjects which of course could easily be grown here. I found the mossy saxifrage on damp rocks up in the hills and butterwort, club moss and some nice ferns. Nothing but ferns and golden rod in the wood and I found *one* Welsh poppy – but that may have been an 'escape'. . . One thing is very pretty here – the seed heads of the bog asphodel – pale salmon-orange all over the swampy part of the hills. . . The chief bore is *wind* – every day – so that hole and corner work with the sketch book is the only practical method as one can't keep one's easel steady.

All the work I have done and that ain't much – seems very scrappy – but I did a fairly finished drawing of a waterfall with large boulders like shiny sultanas covered in moss – a most depressing and eerie place in a silent wood with no sign of even a bird – only 4 in. black slugs creeping around.'

A letter to us both from Laugharne Castle written during a wet August day sometime later in the 1950s begins:

'It needs considerable effort to start a letter on such revolting paper even to dear ones like you but the resources of this small burgh are very meagre and added to this is an air of ineffectual drowsiness that clogs one's outlook, a comatic miasma, so to speak, and all energy is sapped. It has been pretty awful weather here, wind and rain and very few bright intervals. Our position here is claustrophobic and the landscape immediately around is not really very interesting. I fear I shall return with a very small 'bag' and very small game in the bag ... it is a lovely house but the castle is too much infested and invested with ivy – all is lush and green – too green and the rocks are the colour of stale whale meat. We look across to the Gower with wistful eyes.'[2]

In the autumn of 1956 in company with Carel Weight and Edward Bawden the Nashes visited Ironbridge in Shropshire. He wrote:

'The Iron Bridge is very handsome but a teazer to draw with three upright supports and five curved spans to every three so that a sideways view is very complicated if you understand me. We dodge about between the showers and somehow I've done three drawings and a bit – but Carel has done an oil painting every day it seems while Edward keeps his work secretly in his room and does not divulge progress. Carel and I play bar billiards every night, but Bawden will not join in these simple diversions.'[3]

I remember, after one of his painting holidays with Edward Bawden, how John Nash described the disconcerting habit Bawden had of looking over his shoulder as he was working and making such remarks as 'Having difficulty with it?' or 'That is a curious viewpoint'. He mentioned this in a letter in the mid-1960s 'Am busy trying to work out my Norfolk gleanings. "Do you think," as Edward B once said "that you can do anything with those notes you have in your book!" (The barb implied) I do think or must certainly hope so!'[4] John Nash used to pretend that he was utterly floored by such comments. In fact they only spurred him on to fresh endeavours.

In one letter he refers to one of his very rare figure paintings:

25

SELBORNE CHURCH watercolour sketch 1949

'Now I must get to work on my Bathing Belles wh. I'm painting from old drawings – and why not? I was commended by Duncan Grant when he stayed with us and am encouraged to go on working.'[5]

Though the work of other artists had such little effect on his own work, John Nash had many close friends among his fellow painters. These included Henry Rushbury, who was the Keeper of drawings at the R.A., Gilbert Spencer, with whom he used to teach at the Royal College of Art and who had been his best man, Duncan Grant, Eric and Tirzah Ravilious, Edward Bawden, Carel Weight, Clive Gardiner, and Sir Cedric Morris, with whom he shared his interest in plants and flowers. Then there was John Duguid who was always known as 'the coach' because of his habit of imparting information. Latterly he extended his friendship to younger painters and particularly to Peter Coker. His most long-standing friend must have been Bobby Bevan whom he had known since Fitzroy Street days when he had met Bevan's father in company with the other Camden Town painters, Harold Gilman and Spencer Gore. Bevan, the most generous of men, had

26

SELBORNE CHURCH pen drawing 1951 from *The Natural History of Selborne*

proved a true friend and a staunch supporter. In fact this could be said of many of John Nash's friends and patrons. He inspired not only affection but the most enduring loyalty. Yet he was in no way 'a gentle parfit knight'; he could be extremely sharp in his observations about things he did not approve of; he was a monumental grumbler and like most good artists, was oblivious to any discomfort he might cause his friends or his wife by his demands.

*   *   *   *   *

I wrote to him in 1967 after his Retrospective Exhibition at the R.A. and got this in return:

'I must write and thank you for your very kind letter about the Show. I've had quite a number from "dear ones" on the subject and can see myself wading through the pile for weeks to come. But "brother brushes" and inner ring dear ones take precedence as their

27

approbation is the most welcome and rewarding. I *should* be happy at the result and cannot complain on the score of Press notices but one is so contrary and the fact is I am feeling dreadfully flat now that it is launched and long to be able to start work again without quite knowing where or what. It's most unsettling and has forced my mind back to the Past without taking any account for the Future. With all that work at the R.A. it might be said "You've really done enough old sod, why not take a rest". But I hate entire rest – besides it's not economically feasible!

Isn't it a shock to hear one's own voice on the T.V.? Fortunately not a thing one is conscious of at the time. E.B. was quick to comment on my "Public School" accent and I was rather taken aback myself! Well it was a wonderful evening and I hope you enjoyed it!'

ONE FOR THE POT
wood engraving for
Christmas card, undated

The letter finishes with a drawing illustrating 'An ill-advised visit to the Minories. Hemmed in by "Great Girls" seeking autographs.'[6]

In the summer of 1968 John and Christine celebrated their Golden Wedding. Lord and Lady Cranbrook gave them a garden party at Great Glemham on a lovely June evening. John Nash wrote to me a few days later:

'One is touched by all this thoughtfulness and generosity which shines like a beacon in an otherwise rather beastly world! The awful damp makes my hands stiff and aching so you must excuse the calligraphy.'[7] This was one of the rare mentions of the arthritis in his hands. In spite of this crippling handicap, the line in his drawings never faltered.

Nineteen sixty-nine came in with a heavy snowfall and John Nash describes how they were snowed in 'and had to be fetched and carried like a couple of old parcels to 2 parties'.[8] It would have taken more than a snowfall to have kept him away from a party, an attitude to life of the 1920s that never left him.

Each year John Nash would work at great pressure to complete his quota of six paintings or watercolour drawings for the R.A. After Sending-in Day he would relax and start work on his garden with such interruptions as were caused by teaching at the Royal College or later at the Colchester School of Art, and his annual course of plant drawing for Jim Bingley at the Flatford Mill Field Centre.

In the autumn he would start painting again. He used to make forays to the Gower or to Skye or to North Wales, or even on one or two occasions to France. This letter was written in mid-September:

'. . . I dashed out to attend to the local landscape as I do about now and went chasing the stubble fire motive. I got about four subjects

28

and am hard at work except for constant visitors. We go to Skye about the end of the month for a short visit . . . I hope I shall see you soon. I must go now and get my blooming young lady gardener some "elevenses" as C. is in Colchester . . .'[9]

In 1973 John Nash was eighty and a birthday party was given for him at the Minories. This was largely sponsored by Bobby Bevan, the Chairman of the museum. The Minories 'do' was followed up by another party at the Bevans' house at Boxted.

'. . . What a lovely evening that was at Boxted so admirably arranged by Natalie[10] – such a relaxation after the rather formal proceedings at the Minories. There I felt ready to sink into the ground with emotion and some embarrassment as the kind tributes came over thick and fast! But it was most kind of Bobby and I really was touched: But gifts first . . . clothing, Booze and Books – in that order were showered on the old sod. I've never had so many presents on any of my 80 birthdays!'[11]

John Nash was a most sociable person. In East Anglia he was surrounded by friends who were only too happy to give him scope for this side of his nature. Apart from his work and his love of music, his other great interest was fishing. It was during the first Aldeburgh Festival that Lord Cranbrook gave John Nash, on the lawns of Great Glemham House, his first lessons in casting a dry fly. This basic instruction was taken to its logical conclusion when John and Christine Nash went up to Banks, the Cranbrooks' little sheep farm in Westmoreland and on a nearby tarn Nash caught his first trout. He had been a coarse fisherman since he was a boy, fishing for pike during the winter and for tench, perch or carp during the summer months. 'However,' as Jock Cranbrook observed, 'once I had initiated him into the mysteries of fly fishing, he took off.' John Nash not only fished the local Essex ponds and reservoirs, but took his rod as far afield as the Island of Skye and to the West Country rivers. The subject was constantly cropping up in his letters. On one occasion, after referring to some formidable old lady in the pub in which they were staying in Shropshire, he wrote:

'. . . and talking of trout I caught two beauties with Clarence Elliot on the way here, one of 1 lb and the other $\frac{3}{4}$ lb just as darkness was descending and one could not see the fly hit the water – most thrilling.' He concluded that letter with: 'I was to give a Landscape Course in Cheltenham but it's been postponed – the reason Foot and Mouth disease – surely a unique one!?'[12]

The even tenor of his life pursued the same pattern and he continued

TWO GIRLS
wood engraving 1922

29

JOHN NASH FISHING ON THE STOUR AT WISTON photographed by Kurt Hutton 1958

conscious of at other times. EB was quick
to comment on my 'Public School' accent
& I was rather taken aback myself!
Well, it was a wonderful evening & I hope
you enjoyed it.

An ill advised visit to the
Minories. Hemmed in by 'Great Girls'
seeking autographs!

Love to you both
yours John

LETTER from John Nash to Griselda Lewis 22 November 1967

to exhibit at the Royal Academy summer exhibitions where his paintings were always among the first to sell.

In the autumn of 1976 the Buxton Mill Gallery at Buxton Lamas put on a show of his watercolour drawings which was a sell-out. There were two private views, one on the Friday night and the other on the following Saturday morning. We drove up for the morning one, to find John and Christine in a state of euphoria. They had been up until two a.m. Apparently it had been a real party. Christine, at the age of eighty-two, still walked like a dancer. She seemed to be floating round the gallery.

Within one month she was dead, dying quickly and gracefully and causing the least possible trouble to anyone. They had been married for fifty-eight years.

★ ★ ★ ★ ★

After Christine's death, Ronald Blythe came to live with John Nash and looked after him devotedly until he became too ill to stay at home. He was moved to St Mary's Hospital in Colchester. He rallied more than once but it was clear he would never return to Bottengoms. He died on 23rd September 1977.

opposite page :
THRESHING watercolour 1914

2

Paintings and flower drawings

John Nash was an artist who made a unique contribution to English landscape painting. Though he was in the tradition of Cotman and the painters of the Norwich School, he revitalized the art by the honesty of his vision, the simplicity of his style and his understanding of the structure not only of the hills and the valleys, but also the botanical structure of trees, plants and flowers. The results of this can be seen in his paintings which are devoid of sentimental association; the paintings are satisfying objects in their own right.

His work was first shown in 1913 when he exhibited in company with his brother Paul at the Dorien Leigh Gallery in South Kensington. London had already become part of the international art scene. This was largely as a result of Roger Fry's Post-Impressionist exhibitions in 1910 and 1912. Cubism, Futurism and Vorticism were in the air and the Camden Town painters were metamorphosing themselves into the London Group.

As a result of the Nashs' exhibition John was invited to join the newly formed London Group. He had had no formal art training for, on the advice of his brother Paul who had been at the Slade, he had attended no art school. Paul Nash in fact had certain reservations about John becoming an artist. In a letter to his friend Gordon Bottomley, written in July 1912, Paul wrote:

> '. . . he is working on the staff of a country paper and gaining experience for a journalistic career. All his abilities lie in that direction and he will tell you his ambition is to be "a man of letters". These drawings [a bundle that Paul Nash had sent to Gordon Bottomley] are as yet his only expression of himself. He is very observant and writes excellent descriptions of things that strike him, always with the same quaint touch you see in these designs.'

In spite of any doubts Paul Nash may have had about his younger brother's artistic talents, he continued to help him in many ways and so did Claughton Pellew. Each year Paul Nash used to go walking in Norfolk with Claughton Pellew who was a Slade friend. In 1912 Paul could not go so Pellew invited John to come with him instead. They walked along the coast, stopping at Sheringham or Cromer or Mundesley or whatever place they had reached by nightfall. Claughton Pellew gave John Nash much useful advice about the importance of making visual notes, though in fact he carried no sketchbook himself, but merely jotted down notes on the backs of envelopes and mainly relied on a well trained memory. 'Not only did I learn a lot from Claughton,' John Nash said, 'but so did Paul. In fact the influence he had on Paul has never been given its due in the many books that have been written about him and his work. Claughton's knowledge and his technique were a long way ahead of either mine or Paul's.' Claughton Pellew was also a skilful wood engraver and was one of the first to introduce this technique to John Nash.

In 1913 John Nash, as a founder member, exhibited with the London Group, as the Camden Town Group, now much enlarged with the addition of the Vorticists, Cubists and others, had become. The first exhibition was at the Brighton Public Art Galleries. It was an odd and ill-assorted mixture. Sickert remarked that the room put aside for the Vorticists 'made him sick' and Wyndham Lewis and Roger Fry would not speak to each other.

John Nash's actual contact with Roger Fry was slight, though Paul worked for Fry at the Omega Workshops in Fitzroy Street. One of the diverse jobs Fry had taken on was to clean and do extensive retouching on one of Mantegna's tempera paintings from the series *The Triumph of Caesar* hanging at Hampton Court.[1] On one particular morning, John accompanied his brother to the palace. Just as Paul was starting work on the painting, Fry came into the room and saw John standing idly by. He turned to Paul and said:

'If your little brother would like to do a job of work today, he can get down on the floor and repaint the feet.'

'So I got down,' John Nash said, 'and with tubes of Dr Colley's Mixture I started work on the toes! I'm not very proud of that episode. Fancy him letting me loose on a painting like that!'

In the following year the first London exhibition of the London Group was held at the Goupil Galleries. John Nash exhibited, in company with Robert Bevan, Charles Ginner and Harold Gilman, the first President. Nash said many years after:

'The only painter apart from Claughton who really gave me practical advice was Gilman. I learned a lot from him. He was a tremendous talker.' In fact it was Gilman who established John Nash's palette and also the way in which he painted. Gilman's advice was to use his oil paint dry, only to use opaque colour (no rose madder) and never to use pure flake white and never to use black. In fact over the years John Nash's methods had slowly matured and he had used ivory black with its warm undertones and even lamp black, the blackest of all the blacks. Gilman's additional and perhaps most valuable piece of advice was to tell John not to paint from nature but only from notes and drawings done on the spot.

In 1915 Gilman, in company with Ginner and Bevan, started the Cumberland Market Group and invited John Nash with E. McKnight Kauffer and C. R. W. Nevinson to show their works.

At the same time John Nash had become very friendly with Frederick Etchells who was a member of the Vorticist Group. This friendship had a bearing on his future work as a wood engraver and illustrator for it was Etchells who in 1927 asked John Nash to illustrate *Poisonous Plants*.

One of the reasons that Harold Gilman took such a keen interest in John Nash was that the young man's work exhibited the qualities that Gilman most admired. These were to be seen in his combination of formalized design, the simple directness of his observation and the clearness of his drawing. There was no fudging of the issues or blurring of the edges. The early John Nash work sometimes looked naïve, yet all these characteristics were there. There is for example a delightful oil painting entitled *Threshing* which he painted in 1915 and which used to belong to his friend Lance Sieveking. It is a simple counterchange design of a steam engine driving a threshing machine with the figures of three or four labourers silhouetted against the light tone of the ricks, which in turn are in contrast with a dark bank of trees. There is a certain artlessness about it. Yet with its flat tones it is a sophisticated painting.

35

THRESHING etching 1922

Roger Fry wrote in 1920: 'The modern movement was essentially a return to the ideas of formal design which had been almost lost sight of in the fervid pursuit of naturalistic representation.'[2] And in his preface to the second Post-Impressionist Exhibition Catalogue, Fry said about these artists: 'They do not seek to imitate form but to create form, not to imitate life but to find an equivalent for life.' *Threshing* is a modern painting. John Nash, without in any way subscribing to the current admiration for Cézanne and the artists who followed him, had forged his own instrument of expression.

Though John Nash is constantly bracketed with his brother Paul, their inspiration was utterly different and the comparison can be over-laboured. Paul was an intellectual and some of his later work shows the inherent weakness of a purely intellectual approach to painting. John's paintings do have an intellectual austerity, yet there is also an earthiness about them. Nothing lush in his work, rather otherwise, as if the flesh had been picked off and one was left with the bare bones of the land-scape. There is no doubt that John Nash was the more observant landscape painter, though some of Paul Nash's paintings such as *Totes Meer or Dead Sea* may outdistance him at another level.

36

THRESHING oil painting 1915

Late in 1916 John Nash joined up in the Artists' Rifles. He was on active service until the end of the following year. C. R. W. Nevinson records meeting John Nash when he was home on leave. Nevinson wrote:

'I shall never forget seeing poor John Nash – still in the ranks – one day at the Sitwells. He was just back from the front line; and, almost unaware of where he was, he yet mechanically behaved as though he was accustomed to dine with intellectuals night by night.'[3]

After his experience of the Ypres salient it is hardly surprising.

Just before John Nash returned from the Western Front, Paul wrote to his parents from Intelligence H.Q.:

'Jack has been miraculously spared in that he did not go over this time, as he was kept back because he is a very useful man. I found the dear old fellow at last after a day's search, looking very well, a bronzed and tattered soldier, with incredible hands, all rough and overgrown with cuticle – his eyes I thought less shy, very blue and bright, thin in the face but not worn or strained; voice rather tired, but giving out the same wit and humour as of old.'

It was as a result of Paul's untiring efforts that at last John was withdrawn from active service and commissioned as an Official War Artist. In May 1918, before starting on his war paintings, he married Christine Kuhlenthal. She was to become not only a wonderful wife but also a great help in his work. She was very musical, a pleasure they were soon to share, for after they were married John taught himself to play the piano.

John Nash had to find somewhere to work on his war paintings. He discussed this with his brother and Paul suggested they should share a studio so that the two families could be close together. For this purpose they hired a large shed at Chalfont Common near Gerrards Cross. In another letter to Gordon Bottomley, Paul gave some hint of what must have seemed to them to be an idyllic state of affairs:

'It is a roomy place with large windows down both sides, an ample studio – here we work. Jack is lately married – a charming girl whom we all adore . . . they live in rooms in a little house next the shed and Bunty and I have a room in the old farm . . . there is a piano so our wives enchant us with music at times through the day. A phantastic existence as all lives seem these days but good while it lasts and should produce something worth while I suppose. France and the trenches would be a mere dream if our minds were not perpetually bent upon those scenes.'[4]

The shed had been used for herb drying; some Belgians had been billeted near there and had worked on the land growing fields of henbane and belladonna. It was in this drug-laden atmosphere that John Nash painted one of the greatest of the first war paintings, a scene based on the Battle of Cambrai called *Over the Top: 1st Artists' Rifles at Marcoing*. When it was shown at Burlington House in 1919, in an exhibition of war paintings, the Colonel commanding the Artists' Rifles tried to buy it for the Regiment. It was Government property however, so eventually John Nash agreed to paint a replica. This he did in the cellars of the Tate Gallery to which the official war paintings had been consigned.

Soon after his wedding, John Nash painted *The Cornfield* (working on it in the herb drying shed). It foreshadowed the direction his work was to take over the next fifty years or so. It is a lovely painting of yellow cornfields and dusty green trees in high summer. Originally it had been bought by Sir Edward Marsh, one of John Nash's first patrons, who gave it to Ivor Novello the actor, on condition that Novello would leave it to the Tate Gallery. It has been in the Tate since Novello's death in 1952.

*   *   *   *   *

John Nash's serious attitude to his painting permitted of little humour, so no people. *Over the Top* was one of his few excursions into figurative painting. His paintings of the Chilterns, the East Anglian farmlands or Bristol Docks are empty of people, but not surrealistically empty, as is the case in a painting by Dali or Wadsworth whose landscapes look as if they had no atmosphere to support life. In a John Nash picture, it just looks as if the farm labourers have knocked off for the day or the dock workers have gone on strike. In fact the reason for this absence of people is that he was searching for formal qualities of line and tone and basic form. If he was drawing or engraving an illustration, that was a different matter. Then he was depicting a happening, 'a lady being sawn in half' or 'a whole village up in arms'. He did not confuse the two sides of his work. To his way of thinking painting and illustration were fundamentally different things.

The formal quality, common to Japanese prints, that can be seen in John Nash's landscapes, is even more apparent in another side of his work, his flower and plant drawings. When John Nash was eight years old, his family had moved from Kensington to Iver Heath in Buckinghamshire. John and Paul were not new to country life, for before this and for some years after, every autumn they visited their Uncle's farm near Wallingford. The farm was set on the Sinodun Ridge which rises

PASSION FLOWERS lithograph from *English Garden Flowers* 1948
By permission of George Duckworth Ltd

GERANIUM ARMENUM pencil drawing *c.* 1946
By permission of Wilfrid Blunt Esq

up to the Wittenham Clumps – to feature later on in many of John's and Paul's paintings.

John Nash's interest in plants had been awakened by a lively young governess, their second (the first had been sacked by their father for her imperfect knowledge of Latin). At Wellington, to avoid playing cricket, he went in for and won the botany prize. In the holidays he made an attempt to establish a flower garden at his father's home at Iver, with scant encouragement from the Recorder of Abingdon, whose main interest outside the Courts and sole horticultural interest was the tending of his croquet lawn. It was not until 1921 when he and Christine bought their first house at Meadle near Princes Risborough that John Nash had a garden of his own. Here he was also able to cultivate the plants and flowers that he wished to draw. He recently wrote:

'After Wellington my gardening fervour seems to have waned until I married and became a garden owner on the edge of the Aylesbury Plain, below the Chiltern escarpment. By now I must have acquired quite a knowledge of plants through reading, visiting friends' gardens and drawing such plants as I attempted to cultivate. Catalogues which were sent gratis in those days were eagerly studied and kept one in touch with gardening topics. I used to keep all mine in the earth closet at the end of the garden where they came in for constant study.'[5]

In writing about John Nash's flower drawings in the introduction to his show at the Minories in 1967, I said:

'If John Nash had never painted a landscape, his reputation as a botanical draughtsman would have made secure his claim to fame. His plant drawings are nearly always beautiful pieces of design and beautiful things in themselves. Again and again in these flower drawings, I have been struck by the truth and the economy of the drawing. You can feel the substance of the plant and whether it is light or heavy, hollow or solid, textured or smooth. He traps the ephemeral quality of a flower before it wilts and withers away. . .'

Yet in these flower drawings there is nothing transitory. The ephemeral quality that he trapped was revealed by his understanding of the exquisite structure of a plant or a flower. He revealed and formalized this basic structure and had no interest in the chance effects of light and shadow.

In his watercolour landscapes, a two-dimensional quality shows again, for there is little recession in these drawings. One's eye happily wanders round and about the designs but never through and into them.

I think that of all his paintings his winter landscapes mean the most to me. The landscapes are empty, cold and still. They are nearly always painted in a sombre half light. On one winter afternoon, not long before he died, he talked to me about this. He said:

'Whenever it snowed, I never wanted to paint it in full sunlight with all those blue shadows. I would wait until the skies had clouded over and the light had become dim. I would then dash out with my sketch book. That dull light brought out all the colours. Brick walls seemed to glow, the lichen on the trees looked that much richer.'

These paintings of winter scenes do not tempt one to walk into them, for life is one thing and art another. Yet they create the illusion of reality, as does just such a scene by Hokusai or any other of the Japanese masters.

John Nash had his first one-man show at the Goupil Gallery in 1921. In 1924 he joined the staff of the Ruskin School of Drawing at Oxford under Sydney Carline. This was a happy experience and lasted for five years, in fact, until Carline's death. In some ways it was a strange experience, for as he had never attended an art school, this was his first entry into such surroundings, and as a tutor not as a student. No doubt he learned much, 'But nothing,' so he said to me, 'to my irreparable disadvantage!'

The consideration of traditional problems of tone and perspective was something his students were curious about. This may have presented an aspect of painting that he had never bothered with.

In the previous year he visited Norfolk and the grounds over which he and Claughton Pellew had walked before the war. He painted various places, including Cromer.

Bath and Bristol, which he first visited in 1925, proved to be real sources of inspiration. In Bristol, where he made several drawings in the docks, he stayed in a little villa in Cornwallis Crescent, kept by two retired gentlemen's servants. He returned to this scene many times over the years. He was particularly fascinated by the paddle steamers belonging to the Campbell Line which used to be moored alongside Hotwells Road.

He made further summer visits to Bath and Bristol during the next three years. During the winter he worked at home and at the first sign of snow, he was painting the garden at Meadle or the nearby hills and woodlands.

43

FROZEN PONDS oil painting 1958
Mrs. Enid Levetus

'By the mid-twenties,' as Frederick Gore wrote in what is undoubt-
edly the best appreciation that has yet been written about John
Nash's work, 'between them, the Nash brothers had altered the
English idea of landscape painting so that it could never be the same
again. . .' Gore also said: 'Later on it became easier to separate the
influence of one or the other. . . Influences are not easy to distinguish
from affinities but I do not doubt that they did change our sensibility
to landscape in a way which we have absorbed and partly forgotten.
John's best early work too must have affected Paul's work with the
clarity of its images in return for Paul's example at the beginning.'[6]

The last sentence about the reciprocity of influences is something that
seems to have been ignored by critics.
John Nash had another successful exhibition at the Goupil Gallery in
1930 and at about that time took the lease of a tiny thatched cottage on

44

WHITELEAF watercolour 1922
By permission of the Victoria & Albert Museum

the Nayland side of Bures. From then onwards the Stour Valley became his main painting ground though he made further excursions to Bath and Bristol.

In the mid-thirties he joined the staff of the Royal College of Art. With a break for the war, he remained on the staff until 1958.

In company with Eric Ravilious, who with Edward Bawden had worked under Paul Nash at the College, John Nash visited Bristol once again in 1938 and painted some most successful watercolours of the Bristol Docks. One, titled *Nocturne, Bristol Docks*, is in the Bristol City Art Gallery. Another of these watercolours called *Britannia* is of three Campbell steamers in line astern, tied up alongside Hotwells Road. It is an interesting design, with subtle mauves and yellows, reproduced in colour in an article on John Nash's work in *The Studio* of May 1939.

In the spring of the same year John Nash and his wife visited the Gower Peninsula in Glamorganshire and were entranced with it. It

45

seemed to them to be as quiet and deserted as an island in the Outer Hebrides. They stayed at Oxwich Bay and John drew the sand dunes, the cliffs and the sea.

Early in 1940 John Nash was appointed Official War Artist to the Admiralty. He was commissioned into the Royal Marines with the rank of Captain. As the result of his wish to be more actively employed in November he was transferred to active service and a month or so later was posted to the staff of the Commander-in-Chief at Rosyth and later to Portsmouth. He was working on camouflage and deception and took his work very seriously, instantly putting aside all thought of painting. In 1944 he was demobilized with the rank of Major. During this year he and Christine bought Bottengom's farmhouse at Wormingford on the borders of Essex and Suffolk.

At Wormingford he was soon creating a garden out of lush, much overgrown terrain and he was getting back to work. In each year up to 1950, he and Christine revisited the Gower Peninsula where he found the sand dunes and the light very much to his taste. In 1950 they made a diversion to North Wales and it was from there that he made one of his rare references to his fundamental aim as a painter:

'Only now, as we are about to leave, have I been trying to tackle the mountains but I find them very illusive [*sic*]. The light passes over them so rapidly picking out bits here and there that it confuses the artist *searching for basic forms*.'[7]

In 1951 he became a Royal Academician. His fame was secure and he was selling practically every painting and watercolour drawing. Two years later he made his first visit to Skye and complained about how green it was. In the following year the Leicester Galleries gave him the first of the two one-man shows that they arranged.

At the end of the summer term of 1958 John Nash retired from the Royal College, but continued his teaching at the Colchester School of Art. He also used to take a course on Plant Illustration at the Flatford Mill Field Centre near East Bergholt.

'This started chiefly with the idea of drawing the British Flora, but a visit to a local garden full of rare bulbs and herbaceous "exotica" led to defections from the original purpose. There was no wish to spurn the humble forms of our native flora, but they stood a poor chance against the riches of colour and the wealth of form provided by the garden exotics. We wanted to draw our plants with some freedom, giving them air and light and even decorative values, but at the same time to conform to the title of our course. The distinction between a good and a bad plant drawing is hard to make. If you look at the plant draughtsman's Bible, Wilfrid Blunt's *Botanical Illustration*, you will find some illustrations which confirm the need for accuracy combined with the spark of a line drawing, as well as much work which may serve its purpose but gives one no feeling of the living subject.'[8]

In 1960, the Leicester Galleries gave John Nash his second show. It was dominated by *A Panorama of Pyramids*, a painting of China clay tips at St Austell. This was a very striking picture, nearly six feet wide. It was bought by the Office of Works, and now hangs in the British Embassy at Washington. Nineteen sixty-seven was the year of John Nash's Retrospective Exhibition at Burlington House. As well as his paintings there were cases showing much of his graphic work and many of the books that he had illustrated. The artist had doubts about the size of the exhibition and one of the Sunday paper critics agreed with him.

'With a painter who has chugged along a single rural track as long as Nash, so large an exhibition is rather like listening to a ball-by-ball commentary by John Arlott of a minor counties cricket match for three days solid.'[9] This acid simile may not have distressed John Nash too much as he was an admirer of John Arlott and an avid watcher of cricket. But the general opinion was summed up by another critic:

'I doubt if we have ever had a finer botanical draughtsman and not many painters now living are as sensitive to the exact look of the seasons.'[10]

The best tribute ever paid to him came a couple of years later. It was a film made by John Read with a very sensitive commentary by Ronald Blythe. The *Sunday Times* television critic did justice to both artist and film-maker when he wrote:

'John Read's heavenly film *John Nash: a painter in the country* leads us to a better understanding of the creative process . . . the old-fashioned simple dignity of John Nash himself emerged and grew and finally became in the strangest sense of all a piece with the organic poise and fecund serenity of the countryside with which he has identified not only his art, but his spirit, in a perfect integration.'[11]

Paul Nash had had the same idea fifty-five years before:

'John Nash seldom looks at a painting and pays no attention to theories; he reads little about painting, and as a subject for reflexion takes no interest in it at all . . . the real source of his landscape painting . . . is the landscape itself.'[12]

47

THE RECITAL from *The Apple* 1920

From 1919 onwards, at the same time as he was developing his skills as a painter, John Nash was pouring out a stream of very funny drawings. He switched to this work from his serious preoccupation of 'searching for basic forms' without, so it would seem, in any way affecting the quality of his painting.

Facing page, 49
Title-page to *The Shepheards Calender* 1930

on page 49
DRAWING IN THE THEATRE from *Land and Water* 1919

The
Shepheards
Calender
by
Edmund
Spenser.

John Nash.

3

Illustrations and wood engravings

John Nash wrote a brief article in 1950 about illustration in the first number of *ARK*, the Journal of the Royal College of Art, which gives some useful pointers to his attitude. He began by saying:

'The best books to illustrate are those written by the illustrator – a matter between him and his artistic conscience. The next best those by defunct authors – the artist and the publisher only are involved. The most difficult those written by living authors – this means either a tripartite conflict or a dangerous two to one against the illustrator.'

In the same article he describes his method of working:

'I myself read a book in a very practical manner, marking passages that appeal to me or present a vivid picture and indulging in periods of research necessitated by the desire for naturalistic details or the exploration of costume. I then read and re-read until an almost traumatic state is induced from which more imaginative ideas proceed.'

It is worth pointing out that as an illustrator John Nash started by drawing theatrical cartoons and continued to do comic work all his life;

LA BOUTIQUE FANTASQUE from *Land and Water* 1919

even his last book *A Natural History of Selborne* had some very funny drawings in it. The significance of this comic touch was recognized early on. Sidney Schiff, writing in 1925, said: 'In much of John Nash's work wit is close to the surface. Gaiety and lightness are rare qualities in pictures and in those of John Nash laughter is never far away. Perhaps that is the secret of their vitality . . .'.[1]

THE BELLE OF NEW YORK from *Land and Water* 1919

Before that, in 1919, Max Beerbohm in the Foreword he wrote to *Dressing Gowns and Glue* looked deeper, and tells us a great deal about the nature of comic art as well as John Nash's particular contribution.

'That a comic drawing should itself be comic seems to be a reasonable demand. Yet it is a demand which few comic draughtsmen meet. Comic drawings, for the most part, are but comic ideas seriously illustrated... Even in serious art the sense of labour should not be obtruded on us. In comic art it is fatal. Lightness, an air of take-it-or-leave-it spontaneity, is needed to conserve fun. Nor is this all. A light, cursory method is not inconsistent with realism. It may suggest men and things rather precisely as they are. That is not fatal; but it is undesirable. What we want, and what John Nash very signally has, is a light method that is extravagant, that is absurd, a method ancillary to a vision of the world not as (at an earnest glance) the world is, but as, for two pins, one fine morning, it just might be, insomuch that the absurdities inherent in even the best of us could no longer be hushed up.'

Before John Nash started drawing theatrical cartoons he had had one comic drawing published by the *Middlesex and Berks Gazette* when he was working for that paper as a cub reporter. He had quite strong views about humorous drawings and a marked distaste for the *Punch* type of humour, as he explained in the last piece he wrote as art critic for *The London Mercury*.[2]

'Among the hosts of illustrators working for the comic papers there are very few comic artists and more artists than comedians. *Punch* would do well to relieve the monotony of its pages more often with the drawings of Mr Bateman. There is a strength and subtlety in Mr Bateman's line which places him far above other illustrators of this nature, while his knowledge and portrayal of types with utmost economy of means is very stimulating: but then he can afford to be realistic also because he is above all a humorist. . . . Mr George Morrow pleases us frequently by his gentle humour and Mr Haselden, a remarkable man, sustains our daily interest in the *Daily Mirror*. Mr Heath Robinson is a master of whimsical invention, but I am not certain if he is not a very skilful engineer and mechanician in disguise – but certainly ingeniously disguised. Of the regular contributors to *Punch* very little need be said, but what a relief it would be if one week *Punch* went quite mad and appeared with its print upside down, or, better still, no print at all, and if all the artists gave free rein to whatever absurdity possessed them that week!'

ERNEST THESIGER in *Saint George and the Dragon* from *Land and Water* 1919

IRENE VANBRUGH
from *Land and Water* 1919

The theatrical drawings were for a magazine called *Land and Water*, which was owned by J. Murray Allison, a talented Australian who was both a poet and a painter. The editor was J. C. Squire and one of the main contributors was Hilaire Belloc. Each week Nash and the paper's theatre critic, the poet W. J. Turner, would visit a different show. They saw *Kissing Time* starring George Grossmith and Phyllis Dare, and Turner pads out his review with some advice about deportment from the actress Fay Compton. It is really worth quoting: 'The other day, walking down the centre of the big Ritz corridor on my way to lunch, my petticoat fell off. Can you imagine anything more trying than such an event in the most conspicuous place at the most crowded moment, in London's most fashionable restaurant?' Her advice in this emergency was: 'Keep cool, forge ahead!'

The high spot of these theatrical outings was a visit to the Russian Ballet with Leonide Massine's production of *La Boutique Fantasque*. They were both entranced by Lopokova, 'whose can-can,' Turner wrote, 'introduced the desired sensuous and voluptuous touch.'

Apart from these evenings out, John Nash was spending every possible moment painting, but in 1919 his first book illustration job was commissioned. This was *Dressing Gowns and Glue* written by Lance Sieveking, who had served in the Artists' Rifles with Paul Nash, who in his turn had introduced him to his brother John.

These funny drawings had one pervading influence – Edward Lear. The Nashes were introduced to Lear by their formidable Aunt Gussie, who used to read Lear's *Nonsense Rhymes* to Paul when he was a child. Aunt Gussie (her proper name and title was the Hon. Augusta Bethell) was the daughter of the first Baron Westbury, who had been Lord Chancellor from 1861 to 1864. She felt she had almost a proprietary right over Lear, for Lear had been greatly in love with her but was too timid to propose and died still loving her. No doubt it was she who presented Lear's *Nonsense* books to the Nash family because John can remember poring over them at an early age.

The Dressing Gowns and Glue drawings by John Nash are practically unknown to most of the present day admirers of his paintings. The reason I have given them as much space as I have is not because they are such funny drawings but because they are so much a part of the man himself. There can be few painters who were so dedicated to their craft, and such dedication implies a seriousness of purpose. In Nash's case it was, however, a seriousness leavened by a great sense of humour. It was something that helped to make him such a rounded character.

In 1919 John Nash was asked to do some drawings in quite a different vein for a supplement to *Illustration*, the House Organ of the Sun Engraving Co., which was edited by Gerard Meynell. It had contributions by both Nash brothers and their friend Rupert Lee. Something of a minor scandal blew up over this because in it Paul Nash (over the initials RD) had written an article praising his own work and that of his brother John.[3] Frank Rutter revealed the originator of the article in *The Arts Gazette* and Wyndham Lewis, who had a hearty dislike of Paul, also recognised this as Paul's handiwork and made a great fuss. After that Paul and Wyndham Lewis were not on speaking terms, though Lewis did not in any way hold it against John, to whom, irascible man though he was, he was always most courteous and considerate.

In 1921, soon after John and Christine Nash had settled into the house at Meadle, the publishers Chapman and Hall asked John Nash to illustrate a book called *The Nouveau Poor* by Belinda Blinders, a pen name that hid the identity of Desmond Coke, exquisite, dandy, patron of the arts. Coke, who had begun his career as a schoolmaster, had graduated to the humble and obscure post of reader for Chapman and Hall. Quite suddenly he came into a fortune, inherited from a hitherto unknown uncle in Australia. The day he heard about his great bequest he arrived at Chapman and Hall's office in a chauffeur-driven Rolls Royce with a carnation in his buttonhole and smoking a Havana cigar.

A GOOD USE FOR THIS BOOK *from Dressing Gowns and Glue* 1919

SOME MEN WERE WORSE from *Dressing Gowns and Glue* 1919

CARRYING TATTERED COLOURS from *The Nouveau Poor* 1921

OUR OLD ARISTOCRACY from *The Nouveau Poor* 1921

HAYMAKING pen drawing from *Illustration* 1920

LANDSCAPE pen drawing from *Art and Letters* 1919

DUCKS ON A POND pen drawing from Poetry Bookshop *Rhyme Sheet* 1921

Desmond Coke was also the author of a number of books including *The Confessions of an Incurable Collector*,[4] and under the same pseudonym of Belinda Blinders, *Sandford of Merton* and *The Chaps of Harton* which were parts of a trilogy that *The Nouveau Poor* completed. With Frank Rutter's guidance he formed a considerable and most valuable collection of contemporary paintings. In *The Nouveau Poor* Nash matched Coke's amusing parody of the work of contemporary women novelists with some very funny drawings of 'bright young things'. In his *Confessions* Desmond Coke made the following prescient remarks:

'If any man desires to emulate them [the wisest collectors] I say: "Buy Paul Nash, John Nash, William Roberts, Duncan Grant, Vanessa Bell, Mark Gertler and – for sculpture – Eric Gill, with that fodder of the stunt press, Epstein." '

In 1924 John Nash had started teaching at the Ruskin School of Drawing in Oxford. Apart from his teaching he was spending most of his time painting. He did, however, illustrate some *Rhyme Sheets* for Harold Monro at The Poetry Bookshop. These were an indication that he was moving away from purely comic drawing, though for one of them, a poem by Alexander Pope, he produced an amusing sketch of 'gossiping courtiers'. In contrast, for William Allingham's *A Memory*, Nash drew two quite formal designs, one of ducks swimming on a pond, the other of a figure reclining by a lake.

57

Wood engravings from Swift's *Directions to Servants* 1925

In the same year Robert Gibbings invited John Nash over to Waltham St Lawrence, which was not far from Meadle. Gibbings was a fellow member of the Society of Wood Engravers. He was an amiable and kindly giant of a man, and had just taken over the running of the Golden Cockerel Press. This was to be John Nash's introduction to the world of Private Press books for Gibbings asked him if he would do a set of cuts for *Directions to Servants* by Jonathan Swift.

John Nash had been experimenting with the wood engraving medium for the previous couple of years. He had made some individual prints which had appeared in the *Monthly Chapbook*, one called 'Three Pigs' and another of a cat sitting in front of a fire, titled 'Common Objects'. He said later that he liked the feel of boxwood and the discipline of the graver. Such instruction as he had had in wood engraving came from Claughton Pellew and from Rupert Lee. The engravings in *Directions to Servants* are effective designs and also delightfully witty

58

illustrations but they are not proficiently engraved. The book itself, like so many Private Press books, was badly printed, the text set in Caslon Old Face, on handmade paper with a surface as unreceptive as sheet tin. For printing the woodcuts the paper must have been damped or the impressions would not have been half as good as they are. Nash used to proof his small blocks in a nipping press; for larger blocks he had to resort to burnishing them with the rounded handle of a hairbrush.

In the next year (1925) John Nash followed up the Golden Cockerel book with a book for Etchells and Macdonald, another limited editions house which traded under the name of Haslewood Books. This was the same Frederick Etchells whom he had met when Etchells was exhibiting at Brighton with the Vorticists. Etchells had given up painting to practise as an architect and for a short time became a publisher in partnership with Hugh Macdonald.

The first book John Nash illustrated for Etchells and Macdonald was an edition of *Ovid's Elegies* translated by Christopher Marlowe and *The Epigrams of Sir John Davies*. One of his first wood engravings of flowers appears here but the engraving is tentative, he is still feeling his way with the medium.

$$\star \quad \star \quad \star \quad \star \quad \star$$

In 1928 Douglas Percy Bliss's *History of Wood Engraving* was published.[5] In it he discussed the relative merits of the work of John and Paul Nash. Bliss wrote:

'The most enterprising among English artists who have interested themselves in wood engraving are the brothers Paul and John Nash. Their clarity and intensity of vision and their strong instinct for pattern are seen at their fullest in their prints. John Nash's work is gentler and more reticent than that of his brother, not tortured with the same daemonic urge. He is more sensitive and whimsical, more interested in natural objects for their own sakes. Podgy old men or languorous cats interest him as men and cats and are not merely shapes and forms.'

Douglas Bliss also makes another perspicacious remark:

'His [John Nash's] sense of humour which enables him *to make the best comic drawings of today* (for he counts it as a relaxation from more serious work and not as a means of earning a living) comes out delightfully in his engravings, notably in the edition of Swift's *Directions to Servants*'.

Wood engravings from Ovid's *Elegies* 1925

INTERIOR OF A WOOD wood engraving 1922

THRESHING wood engraving 1925

SHEEP SHEARING wood engraving 1922

QUIET EVENING wood engraving 1924. The models are Christine and Barbara Nash

Bliss's comments must have pleased John Nash. He was able to read them before the book was on the market, for Jack Squire asked him to review it for the *London Mercury*. He enjoyed writing and has always written with a mixture of decorum and wit, which comes out more in his letters than in his published work. His review of Douglas Bliss's book is a thoughtful piece of prose. In discussing the nature of wood engraving, he wrote:

'We hear so much about spontaneity, it is much to be desired in mediums which lend themselves to it. The brush or the pencil can be

COMMON OBJECTS wood engraving 1924

loosely controlled but the graver cannot be handled loosely, no flourishes are possible. Engraving demands a tight control and respectful deliberation. Moreover, the design must be carefully planned out beforehand and the engraver should know exactly what he is about to do within the limits of the block. Here chance or extempore decisions, happy or otherwise, are the last elements to depend on.'

THORN APPLE wood engraving from *Poisonous Plants* 1927

He never liked the idea of producing prints for framing and expressed this point of view quite forcefully.

'It is in the illustration of books, the ideal combination of type, block and the printed page, that the future of wood engraving would seem to lie . . . as wall decorations they compete unsuccessfully, I think, with easel paintings and drawings, owing to the lack of colour and

HORNED POPPY wood engraving from *Poisonous Plants* 1927

limited size, and are, therefore, more suitable for portfolios, but the use of them in books provides an aim worth achieving, a two-fold aim of decoration and illustration . . . it is as well to be alive to the dangers like those that have beset the etching world where many etch, and skilfully, but few have anything to etch about.'[6]

John Nash had plenty to engrave about, though to a less able botanical draughtsman the attempt to portray the fragility of leaves and petals might have seemed an impossible subject for the graver. John

66

SPURGE LAUREL wood engraving from *Poisonous Plants* 1927

Nash took this in his stride not only in *Poisonous Plants* but also with engravings for several other books, notably *Flowers and Faces*.

The books produced by Etchells and Macdonald are worthy of more attention than they have so far received from collectors. They produced three of the most distinguished illustrated Press Books of the time. These were *Eve's Legend* by Lord Holland, where the text was written with the letter 'e' being the only vowel present; it had engravings by Hester Sainsbury who became the second Mrs Etchells. *Eve's Legend* was followed by *Sailing Ships and Barges of the Western Mediterranean and*

HERB PARIS wood engraving from *Poisonous Plants* 1927

Adriatic with copper engravings by Edward Wadsworth. Thirdly in 1927 came *Poisonous Plants* by W. Dallimore with wood engravings by John Nash. Here Nash comes into his own. These rich, black cuts have the authority of a very skilled draughtsman, a working botanist and an engraver who had gone far to master his craft. Not long before he died Nash remarked that he would have liked to redesign some of these engravings; but the best of them, those of the thorn apple, the foxglove, daphne and herb Paris, will stand in any company.

Later in life John Nash had something more to say about *Poisonous Plants*. In *The Artist Plantsman*[7] he wrote:

'The actual title of the book was *Poisonous Plants: Deadly, Dangerous and Suspect*. The publishers thought that someone "with a name" should be asked to write an introduction, so the Director of Kew was invited to do this, but in the end Dr Hill merely lent his name and delegated the plant descriptions to a member of his staff. I was left to write the introduction myself which gave me the added pleasure of being both artist and author.'

Poisonous Plants is a very handsome book, beautifully printed by the Curwen Press on a smooth, creamy vellum-like paper. Etchells and Macdonald had planned to follow up *Poisonous Plants* with a book on carnivorous plants. John Nash actually did one engraving, but the idea was shelved and soon after that the firm closed down.

In 1929 John Nash engraved a single illustration for the Cresset Press edition of *The Apocrypha*. This was illustrated with engravings by a number of widely differing artists, including René Ben Sussan, Gertrude Hermes, Blair Hughes Stanton and Eric Ravilious. Nash's

A House in the Country 1927
wood engraving used for a book jacket

Anatomy of Dessert 1929
wood engraving used for a book jacket

engraving was for the book of *Judith*, a somewhat macabre subject that can hardly have been to his taste. He also engraved illustrations for two more Golden Cockerel books and a charming little book called *Céleste*.

Céleste was published by the Blackamore Press and written by his friend Sidney Schiff (under the pen name of Stephen Hudson). Schiff came from a rich banking family. He was a man-about-town, an entrepreneur and one of John Nash's early patrons. Having been seen everywhere Schiff suddenly disappeared. Some time later, according to John Nash, Osbert Sitwell met him one day by chance in Piccadilly and said:

'Where have you been Sidney? We haven't seen you at parties for months.'

'No,' replied Schiff with a curiously self-satisfied smirk, 'and the reason is I have put all my eggs into one lovely basket.' Sitwell was

FRAU KARL DRUSCHKI wood engraving from *Céleste* 1930   TRANSMUTATION wood engraving from *Céleste* 1930

quite nonplussed but apparently Schiff was referring to his new wife.

In 1930, in addition to illustrating *Céleste* with wood engravings, John Nash illustrated Edmund Spenser's *The Shepheards Calender* and Cobbett's *Rural Rides*, both with pen drawings. *The Shepheards Calender* was the first serious book, apart from Clarence Elliott's catalogue, that John Nash had illustrated in line. It was published by Denis Cohen at the Cresset Press. The line drawings were hand coloured which gave them a pleasant freshness. This is further enhanced by a certain naïvety in the drawings. To achieve a satisfactory result the line drawings were reproduced and proofed in black; the artist then coloured the proofs. From these hand-coloured proofs stencils were cut and watercolour was then applied for each colour on the printed sheets. This stencil process (the French call it *pochoir*) gave a quality to the printed page far superior to any halftone process, but because of the hand work involved

71

TWO TUGS wood engraving 1929

it was not a cheap method. The work was done by the Curwen Press. The book was printed on Barcham Green's handmade, deckle-edged grey paper, which was none too sympathetic.

In the year before the publication of *Poisonous Plants* John Nash had done some additional drawings for a new edition of Sieveking's *Dressing Gowns and Glue*, this time called *Bats in the Belfry*. This was a more substantial volume but still contained the original introductions by G. K. Chesterton who wrote about the verse, and Max Beerbohm's essay about comic drawings.

In 1926 John Nash had been approached by Clarence Elliott, a nurseryman and horticulturist, who was destined to become one of the artist's closest friends. They shared two overriding interests, the cultivation of rare plants and fishing. Elliott had the idea that if his catalogues were illustrated he might be able to sell them. To this end John Nash drew a number of illustrations which he and Christine coloured by hand. 'We sweated blood over them,' he said. The catalogues were priced at ten shillings each and quickly sold out.

HE'S BATS-IN-THE-BELFRY, POOR CHAP! from *Bats in the Belfry* 1926
By permission of Routledge and Kegan Paul Ltd

WHEN M.A'S AVERT THEIR GAZE from *Bats in the Belfry* 1926
By permission of Routledge and Kegan Paul Ltd

The third book to appear in 1930 with John Nash's illustrations was the very handsome edition of Cobbett's *Rural Rides*. This was published by Peter Davies (one of J. M. Barrie's godchildren). The only fault one can find with this book is that the line illustrations are too thinly scattered through the three volumes. To some degree they foreshadow John Nash's illustrations for *Selborne*. One or two of them are very funny, yet they are decorative and rather formal in design, drawn in a technique comparable to that used by line engravers, with a fair amount of cross hatching. This was to be the pen technique he used for his book illustrations for the rest of his life.

In 1930 John Nash also designed a lorry bill (poster) for Jack Beddington at Shell-Mex. His brother Paul had already done a successful Shell lorry poster of Rye marshes. John's design was of the Dundas aquaduct over the River Avon but Beddington did not like it and it was never published.

John Nash repeated the line and stencil colour treatment that he had used in *The Shepheards Calender* for *Seven Short Stories* by Walter de la Mare, which Faber published in 1931. For this book, which was printed by the Curwen Press, Barnett Freedman did the separations. Freedman was himself a distinguished artist and lithographer. (See pages 80-81.)

The drawings in *Seven Short Stories* are very strange and perfectly match the weird tales. There is one, a night scene of a wood lit by a crescent moon illustrating the story 'Bird of Travel', which is a coldly pretty design. It has been reproduced in colour at least twice,[8] but there are others in this book which are just as effective. There is another night scene, this time with a full moon, illustrating 'The Tree'; two anonymous, bowler-hatted figures, a cabman and his fare, stand by a blown horse staring across a hedgerow at a tree. Another drawing that is quite surrealist illustrates 'Maria-Fly'. Here is a close-up of a house-fly drawn many times larger than the little girl who sits watching it. The semi-overhead viewpoint produces an almost Japanese effect. The simple colours used in these illustrations, a slightly washed-out blue, a dusty pink and a Naples yellow, combine with an even weight of line in cross hatched or parallel line shading to produce the most unpretentious technique of illustration imaginable. *Seven Short Stories*, modestly produced book though it may be, is a triumph of the illustrator's art.

John Nash's second book for the Golden Cockerel Press was *When thou wast naked* by T. F. Powys, for which he did five woodcuts, including a particularly pretty one of two girls up an apple tree. In the same year (1931) he provided four coloured plates for *The New Flora and Silva*, a quarterly run by Ewan Cox for the horticultural world. He also illustrated in line *One Hundred & One Ballades* for Cobden Sanderson, a commercial publisher whose books were often much more elegant

SHAVING THE BARK OFF THE HOP POLES
pen drawing from *Rural Rides* 1930

THE EVER-DAMNED POTATOES
pen drawing from *Rural Rides* 1930

YOU GO THROUGH HOLLOW WAYS
pen drawing from *Rural Rides* 1930 ▶
By permission of Peter Davies Ltd

KENTISH APPLES
pen drawing from *Rural Rides* 1930

A ROMAN DAME HAS JUST BEEN SAWN IN TWO pen drawing from *One Hundred and One Ballades* 1931

THE PELLETS FROM MY AIRGUN WENT ASTRAY pen drawing from *One Hundred and One Ballades* 1931

and tasteful than the more pretentious offerings of the Private Presses.

In *One Hundred & One Ballades* the nineteen pen drawings, mostly depicting some personal disaster, are very funny. Among the funniest is one illustrating a line by G. K. Chesterton 'That brutalising Billiard Show', of snooker players with expressions of extreme annoyance on their faces, pelting each other with billiard balls; another illustrates:

> 'A Dean of Ashton-under-Lyne
> Lives wholly upon new-mown hay'

with a portly dean down upon his knees in front of a hay cart stuffing himself with hay, to the dismay of the carthorse and the manifest surprise of the carters. There is yet another and even funnier one illustrating:

> 'A Roman dame has just been sawn in two
> (– She mocked Il Duce in a villanelle.)'

In this drawing the two halves of the unfortunate lady are whirled up into the air by a steam-driven circular saw whilst *il Duce* and his beady-eyed guard of honour salute the event with their hands held high in the air. The best thing in the picture is the look of haughty disbelief on the noble matron's face.

Wood engraving from *When thou wast naked* 1931

GARDEN FLOWERS pen drawing from *The Curious Gardener* 1932
By permission of Faber and Faber Ltd

HELLEBORUS CORSICUS pen drawing from *The Curious Gardener* 1932
By permission of Faber and Faber Ltd

Commissions for more flower drawings followed this excursion into humour. The first of these was *The Curious Gardener* by Jason Hill, published by Faber in 1932. 'Jason Hill' hid the identity of Dr Anthony Hampton, a close friend of John and Christine Nash from the 1920s. This was followed by a series of plant drawings for *The Listener* to illustrate articles also written by Jason Hill. These were later produced in book form under the title of *The Contemplative Gardener*.

THE BIRD OF TRAVEL line and colour pochoir drawing from
Seven Short Stories 1931
By permission of Faber and Faber Ltd

THE TREE from *Seven Short Stories* 1931
By permission of Faber and Faber Ltd

MARIA-FLY line and colour pochoir drawing from *Seven Short Stories* 1931
By permission of Faber and Faber Ltd

SPRING FLOWERS wood engraving from *Flowers and Faces* 1935

CANTERBURY BELLS AND OTHER SUMMER FLOWERS wood engraving from
Flowers and Faces 1935

The last set of illustrations that John Nash engraved were for his
third Golden Cockerel Press book *Flowers and Faces* by H. E. Bates.
These wood engravings illustrated the four seasons and there was also a
decorative frontispiece. The artist regarded these as his best engraved
work, 'particularly from the point of view of precision,' he said. He had
certainly mastered the medium, and having mastered it he became

MARROW AND OTHER AUTUMN FRUIT AND FLOWERS wood engraving from
Flowers and Faces 1935

bored with it and so forsook the graver for the pen and lithographic
chalk. After the completion of *Flowers and Faces* he never did another
engraving.

The prints in *Flowers and Faces* are certainly beautiful things, rich,
black and velvety in spite of the same old hard and unsympathetic
handmade paper. There is one marvellous print, a harvest festival

subject with a huge striped vegetable marrow, tomatoes, apples and pears overhung with a giant sunflower, dahlias and Michaelmas daisies; it made a fine farewell to the art of wood engraving.

In fact there was more to it than boredom to make him give up engraving on the wood. One of the main sources of commission for engravings was the Private Presses, and they had nearly run their course. Also engraving on wood is a most laborious and time-taking method of illustration and John Nash had perfected a technique for drawing in line that would suit any subject he liked to tackle. He could do three or four line drawings in the time it took to do one wood engraving.

*   *   *   *   *

Some time in the early 1930s John Nash was taken to one of Lady Ottoline Morrell's parties at Garsington. There he met Robert Gathorne-Hardy. They soon discovered their common interest in gardening. This common interest resulted in John Nash illustrating Gathorne-Hardy's *Wild Flowers in Britain*, which Batsford published in 1938. The Nash illustrations for this book (there were also photographs) are a mixture of auto-lithographs and pen drawings. The lithographs inside the book are less successful than the pretty lithographed wrapper design.

These were the first lithographic illustrations that Nash had done for a book, although two of his early lithographs appeared in *The Golden Hind*,[9] one of Christine Nash asleep on a sofa and another of some farm buildings. He had had some instruction in the craft in the early 1920s from that sensitive artist Francis Unwin, who had been introduced to him at the Goupil Gallery by Alan Durst. Unwin in fact had suggested that John Nash should come up to his studio in Hampstead where he could try his hand at drawing on the stone.

It was not long after this that Unwin's lifelong fight against tuberculosis made it necessary for him to re-enter a sanatorium at Mundesley in Norfolk where in 1925 he died. Mark Gertler was a fellow patient and in fact witnessed Unwin's will a few days before his death. In that will he bequeathed all his etchings to the Print Room at the British Museum. Before he died he gave John Nash his motor car, the first car that Nash owned. It was an 8.18 hp Talbot, an expensive little car 'in which,' so John Nash recalled, 'Unwin used to go tootling round Brooklands'. In 1928 John Nash had edited *Francis Unwin, Etcher and Draughtsman* for the Fleuron.

85

Pen drawings from *Men and the Fields* 1939
By permission of B. T. Batsford Ltd

In the autumn of 1938 Nash was illustrating Patrick Synge's *Plants with Personality*. This book, published by Lindsay Drummond, is a curious compound of photographs, monochromatic reproductions from Thornton's *Temple of Flora* and eight very good botanical line drawings by John Nash, who regarded them as amongst the best flower drawings he had ever done.

In 1939 John Nash illustrated another book for Batsford. This was *Men and the Fields* by Adrian Bell. There are six not very successful

Pen drawings from *Men and the Fields* 1939
By permission of B. T. Batsford Ltd

lithographs and some line drawings which are as assured as the lithographs are tentative.

All in all, *Men and the Fields* is still an attractive book. The drawings are considerably reduced, with the effect that they could easily be mistaken for copper engravings. *Men and the Fields* was the last book that Nash illustrated before he became involved in the war.

John Nash, like several other painter-designers of his generation, was associated with the Curwen Press. He was introduced to Oliver Simon

Pen drawings from *Men and the Fields* 1939
By permission of B. T. Batsford Ltd

Pen drawing from *Men and the Fields* 1939
By permission of B. T. Batsford Ltd

at Curwen by his brother Paul. Probably as a result of this it was the Curwen Press that printed from electrotypes his *Poisonous Plants* and printed it very well. The engraving of Black Bryony was used by the Curwen Press in 1935 to advertise an Evensyde printing paper for John Dickinson. The black engraving was effectively framed in one of Edward Bawden's typographic borders, printed in red.

This was not the first use of a Nash engraving for advertising, for in 1928 he engraved an illustration of a tobacco plant to advertise Southern Rhodesian tobacco. Such other work as he did for Curwen was by lithography, including a cover for the Curwen Press *Newsletter No 14* in 1937 and a frontispiece for *Signature No 12* in 1939, though this was actually printed under the guidance of T. E. Griffits at the Baynard Press for whom it was intended to be an advertisement.

In 1937 he drew a large lithograph *The Stour at Bures*, which was published by Contemporary Lithographs. His last work to be printed at the Curwen Press was *Men and the Fields*. The most successful results that Curwen achieved from John Nash's illustrations were not the auto-lithographs but the wood engravings in *Poisonous Plants* and the stencil reproductions for the Cresset Press edition of *The Shepheards Calender* and Walter de la Mare's *Seven Short Stories*.

JULY from *Almanack of Hope* 1944
By permission of The Bodley Head

JANUARY from *Almanack of Hope* 1944
By permission of The Bodley Head

The first book that John Nash was asked to illustrate after he was demobilised in the autumn of 1944 was a little book of poems by John Pudney, A. P. Herbert's son-in-law, called *Almanack of Hope*. It was a typical example of wartime austerity production, but the drawings match the title. They are a paean, an absolute chant of thanksgiving that the war should be nearing its end.

For the next couple of years John Nash did little illustration. When he was not painting his time was taken up with converting a wilderness into a garden of rare beauty. But there were problems involved with living in such a remote and primitive cottage. There were many days during the first two winters at Bottengoms when it was too cold for him to work either in the garden or in the studio.

OCTOBER from *Almanack of Hope* 1944
By permission of The Bodley Head

SEPTEMBER from *Almanack of Hope* 1944
By permission of The Bodley Head

In 1947 John Nash drew two of the illustrations for the Cowell typebook. One was of Bristol docks (which is reproduced here on page 19). The second of the two drawings was to illustrate Gilbert White's letter about the tortoise from *The Natural History of Selborne*. This little typebook had a considerable success, mainly because of the quality of the illustrations.

In the following year John Nash drew some lithographs for Mervyn Horder at Duckworths, who published them under the title of *English Garden Flowers*. These lithographs are an advance on those in *Men and the Fields* but lithography was never Nash's medium. They are competent, yet lack both the charm and the incisive bite of his pen drawings or his woodcuts.

Pen drawing from the back cover of *Five graves at Nijmegen* 1945

I asked John Nash what he now felt about his lithographs. His forthright reply more than confirmed my feelings.

'I strove nobly and long, but I never mastered the craft,' he replied 'I am afraid I agree with you, they are mostly not much good.'

In a comment in the Cowell typebook about John Nash's *Selborne* drawing I wrote: '. . . it would be a pleasant thought if some enterprising publisher was to give our foremost flower painter the task of illustrating this classic'. It was bread on the waters. Two years later Joscelyn Oliver wrote to tell me the Lutterworth Press was going to ask John Nash if he would undertake this task. He also asked me to write an introduction to the book.

John Nash was a deceptively professional illustrator. In the November of 1950 he wrote to me about the progress of *Selborne*:

'I visited the Lutterworth Press last week to find out what progress was being made in the matter of White's *Selborne* as I was afraid that it might quite likely appear suddenly without our first having seen

THE MOOSE pen drawing from *The Natural History of Selborne* 1951

HARVEST MICE pen drawing from *The Natural History of Selborne* 1951

ROCKY LANE NEAR THE LITHE pen drawing from *The Natural History of Selborne* 1951

either proofs of the drawings or the title-page. As I suspected J——
had thought of sending me proofs but did not as he fancied I could not
bear to see them on the usual shiny proof paper and so did no more –
As if I had never seen proofs of this kind before and could not make
allowances! I got from him a file proof of the whole book and found
five drawings omitted – however, this is to be rectified and they are to
be used for end pieces. The drawings look pretty well and the title-
page seems inoffensive to my untutored eye.'[10]

He never stood any nonsense from printers or publishers and such
was his air of moral rectitude that he always got his way.

The Nash *Selborne* appeared in 1951. To save money the pen drawings

96

I HAVE KNOWN A WHOLE VILLAGE UP IN ARMS from *The Natural History of Selborne* 1972

CORNFIELD BELOW THE HANGER pen drawing from *The Natural History of Selborne* 1951

were produced without additional colour. The book was in fact a fairly economical production. The drawings were brilliant, but I felt at the time that they would have been even better with colour. There was to be a sequel to this thought, but that was some twenty or more years ahead. In fact it was in 1972 that the Limited Editions Club published *The Natural History of Selborne* with John Nash's illustrations.

For this new edition John Nash took his original line drawings that had been used for the Lutterworth edition and added flat colours to them. The labour of doing the separations was too much for him because of the increasingly arthritic state of his hands, so a sympathetic and skilful young artist called Pamela Mara undertook this work after he had hand-coloured a set of proofs. The result is a very beautiful book.

THE NIGHT-JAR pen drawing from *The Natural History of Selborne* 1972

SELBORNE HANGER pen drawing from *The Natural History of Selborne* 1972

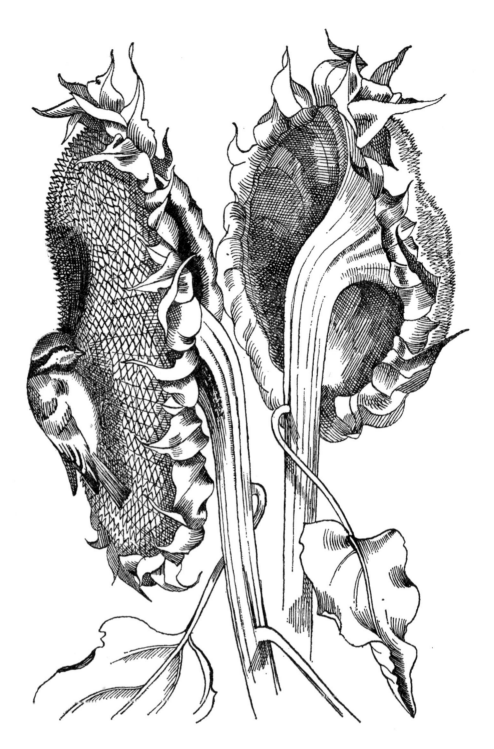

WELL ENTERTAINED WITH A SUNFLOWER pen drawing from *The Natural History of Selborne* 1972

STREAM IN THE LITHE pen drawing from *The Natural History of Selborne* 1972

With the addition of colour the drawings take on quite another dimension. The drawings are also reproduced nearer to the size he drew them, so the two Selborne editions appear to be quite different books. Of the coloured illustrations, those that gain most from this enrichment are the landscapes such as 'Stream in the Lithe' or the botanical studies such as 'Stinking Hellebore'. The most amusing drawing in both coloured and black and white versions is of a moonlit scene of armed yokels in a churchyard illustrating a letter about white owls. It is called: 'I have known a whole village up in arms'. It is not only a very funny drawing but it is a beautiful design as well.

Lord Cranbrook in his introduction to the Limited Editions Club *Selborne* says: '. . . these witty and observant drawings are worthy of Gilbert White's great and enduring book . . . between 1919 and 1971 John Nash has illustrated more than thirty books and amongst these his *Selborne* must stand supreme'. It is indeed a splendid swansong to his work as an illustrator.

THE LOVER AT THE DOOR pen drawing from *Parnassian Molehill* 1953
By permission of W. S. Cowell Ltd

In 1953 Cowells (in the person of Geoffrey Smith) re-entered the publishing field with *Parnassian Molehill*. This was a witty anthology of Suffolk verse compiled by another close friend of the artist, the Earl of Cranbrook, a naturalist of some repute and Bob Gathorne-Hardy's elder brother. It was illustrated in line by John Nash and was a most happy collaboration. The line drawings are a mixture of studies of flowers and animals and comic illustrations of cuckolded husbands, drunken revellers and snowballing lovers. There is also a drawing of a

Tailpiece pen drawing from *Parnassian Molehill* 1953
By permission of W. S. Cowell Ltd

OF A SNOW BALLE pen drawing from *Parnassian Molehill* 1953
By permission of W. S. Cowell Ltd

hooked fish being landed in a net, a reminder that both he and the anthologist shared a passionate interest in fishing, both coarse and fly.

The reviewer in the *Times Literary Supplement* wrote: 'The binding of the book [a repeating pattern of roses drawn by John Nash] is exquisite, the paper bland, the typography dignified, while the pictorial comments by John Nash are sometimes Arcadian and sometimes comic. It is a molehill worthy of Parnassus.'[11]

UFFOLK! ONE BUMPER TO THY HORSE pen drawing from *Parnassian Molehill* 1953
By permission of W. S. Cowell Ltd

JULY pen drawing from Benham's Calendar 1958

In 1957 John Nash was asked by Tom Hart, the managing director of Benhams, the Colchester printers, if he would illustrate a calendar for them. The result was a set of quite beautiful line and colour drawings. The year begins with one of his favourite subjects, a snow-covered, gently undulating landscape with an icy pond in the foreground, with frost blackened rushes; in the distance a path leads up to a leafless coppice and the whole scene is lit by a wintry sun. John Nash takes us through the year with drawings of the countryside, of old-fashioned roses, of girls bathing, of blackberries ripening and for November a striking design of a fisherman hooking a pike.

NOVEMBER from Benham's Calendar 1958

SEPTEMBER from Benham's Calendar 1958

Though these designs for Benhams were intended to be printed with colour, the colours are mostly muted, as in the November picture of the fisherman, yet they stand up perfectly well to being reproduced in line alone. The roadside scene on this page of swallows gathering on the telegraph wires with a close-up view of the Greater Bindweed, or the

105

OCTOBER pen drawing from Benham's Calendar 1958

drawing of the blackberries above are complete pen drawings. One feels
the colour is almost irrelevant. John Nash was not a colourist, and
sometimes when he used local colour, such as a violent red in the
combine harvester design, it throws the drawing out of key.

In the same year he also wrote and illustrated an article for John

106

Hadfield's *The Saturday Book*. It was called 'Cottage Window Plants'.
'or this he drew a Scarborough lily, a pelargonium, an epiphyllum, a
variegated aloe and a very funny drawing of himself and Clarence
Elliott peering through a cottage window at a magnificent *Campanula
isophylla* behind which stood an irate bearded householder.

107

ADMIRING A PARTICULARLY FINE SPECIMEN pen drawing from *The Saturday Book* 1957

CHRISTMAS CARD pen drawing 1958

THE FARMHOUSE WINDOW advertisement drawing for Crittalls 1958

In addition to book illustration John Nash designed a number of book jackets, using both lithography and, in the early ones, wood engravings. He also did several jobs for advertising, including a fine pen drawing for Crittalls. Among other advertising jobs were the cover designs for the Shell Guides for Dorset and Cambridgeshire.

In September 1958 John Nash wrote to me in his modest vein about some drawings he was doing for the cover of *The Countryman* magazine which, through his good offices, I was redesigning for John Cripps:

'But to business. Here is a copy of *The Countryman* with the space proposed for embellishment $3\frac{1}{2} \times 2\frac{1}{2}$in. I also enclose my existing roughs looking rather horrid I fear as I have got in the habit of using this Biro type for preliminary work. I would welcome any comments

OLD FASHIONED ROSES pen drawing from *The Tranquil Gardener* 1958
By permission of Thos. Nelson and Sons Ltd

– i.e. as to whether you think these will be strong enough when translated into terms of black and white or rather black and green. I think I shall have to do them twice the size in order to give myself space for manoeuvring and simplification of such tonal cross hatching as is proposed.'[12]

He illustrated two more books by Bob Gathorne-Hardy. The first of these was *The Tranquil Gardener* (1958), which the author 'Dedicated

CACTUS AND SUCCULENTS pen drawing from *The Tranquil Gardener* 1958
By permission of Thos. Nelson and Sons Ltd

with all the affection of a very old friendship and the unwavering
fervour of an early admiration to John Nash, the felicities of whose art
will in this book redeem any shortcomings of my own'. The illustrations
consist of four watercolours reproduced by offset and twenty-eight line
drawings which must be among the best flower drawings he ever did.
The second book by Gathorne-Hardy was *The Native Garden* (1961)
which, like *The Tranquil Gardener*, was published by Joscelyn Oliver at
Nelsons. It contained some very pretty watercolour drawings of groups

ALTHAEA OFFICINALIS: MARSH MALLOW from *The Native Garden* 1961
By permission of Thos. Nelson and Sons Ltd

of flowers as well as many fine pen drawings, which by their economy of line reveal with clarity the structure and texture of leaves and flowers.

In 1958 the Shell Chemical Company launched a magazine called *Land* about farming and allied subjects. The editor of this magazine was David Wolfers, a man of artistic sensibility who was later to become the founder and director of the New Grafton Gallery. *Land* featured the work of many twentieth-century artists, including Robert Bevan, Paul

RUSCUS ACULEATUS: BUTCHER'S BROOM from *The Native Garden* 1961
By permission of Thos. Nelson and Sons Ltd

Nash, Elinor Bellingham-Smith, Robert Buhler and John Nash. The first number in fact had as a cover design a reproduction of a water-colour of a ploughed field by Paul Nash. John Nash's painting 'Frozen Ponds' was reproduced on the cover of the Winter number in 1958.

In 1959 he made a series of comic drawings for *Happy New Lear*, a sixteen-page booklet for Guinness. The originator of this amusing little offering was his friend Bobby Bevan, then Chairman of S. H. Benson.

'THEY ARE THE BEST FRIENDS A FARMER CAN HAVE'

'SEEM TO DEVELOP A SORT OF HIERARCHICAL PECK-ORDER'

'THE HALCYON DAYS WHEN THE DOGS LAY PANTING' from The Stack-dwellers
Land 1962

On a winter's day early in 1960 Nash visited a farm near Lowestoft in
company with David Wolfers and did numerous drawings to illustrate
an article about this farm, including one of reed beds which was
reproduced in colour. He wrote to me about these drawings:

'I'm usually rather free and dashing with the $\frac{1}{2}$-tone wash in my
sketches, but these seem a little stilted and maybe I should have kept to
the old cross-hatching only.'

In the Spring number of *Land* for 1962 John Nash illustrated an
article about rats and mice by Lord Cranbrook. This was a return to
the days of his comic drawing. There are only three illustrations but
they are as amusing as any he ever did. The scene of a steam-driven
threshing machine might have been drawn on any day in the previous
fifty years. He was nothing if not consistent.

115

JUNE pen drawing from *The BBC Book of the Countryside* 1963

These comic drawings were followed by another set of funny drawings for *Thorntree Meadows* by Roger Nett, an American author, which once again had Joscelyn Oliver at Nelsons as publisher. This was, in fact, John Nash's last piece of comic illustration apart from the Christmas cards that he drew every year. In 1965 he illustrated for

116

JULY pen drawing from *The BBC Book of the Countryside* 1963

Evans Brothers *The Art of Angling* in collaboration with David Tuhill, one of his former students.

The BBC Book of the Countryside is a month-by-month anthology, illustrated by a number of artists, including Sheila Robinson, Walter Hoyle and John Nash. For this book Nash did six drawings, varying in

Pen drawings from *The Art of Angling* 1965

subject matter from a comic drawing of carol singers for December, to the two fine drawings here, the one of netted strawberries and currant bushes is for June, the other of lilies, peonies and old fashioned roses is for July.

*　　*　　*　　*　　*

The subtitle to this book about John Nash is 'The painter as illustrator'. The best comment about this was made by Philip Hofer in 1961 in his introduction to *The Artist and the Book 1560–1960*, the catalogue of an exhibition at the Museum of Fine Arts, Boston, in which John Nash's *Poisonous Plants* was exhibited. Philip Hofer wrote:

'. . . now that the artist is well paid for his work – as professional illustrators have usually not been – a rapidly growing number of the most talented painters and sculptors have become attracted to the arts of the book. This quite startling recent evolution is particularly evident on the continent of Europe which has, as usual, followed the lead given by France. It is not yet apparent in the Anglo-Saxon world of Great Britain and America, where a prejudice against "book illustration", long held to be a minor art form, has been strongly entrenched.'

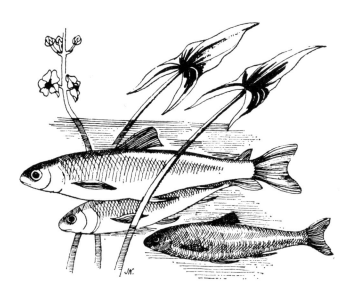

Pen drawings from *The Art of Angling* 1965

Hofer's observations about prejudice against book illustration are certainly true and few English painters have tackled book illustration. If they have it has usually been in their early struggling days. As soon as they have achieved success with their paintings they have shied away from such lowly work. In the last century the Pre-Raphaelite painters Edward Burne-Jones, John Everett Millais and Dante Gabriel Rossetti illustrated a number of books, but only Burne-Jones continued with the craft and that was on the lofty level of the Kelmscott Press.

The one nineteenth-century painter-illustrator who has much in common with John Nash is Edward Lear who painted landscapes, made comic drawings and illustrated fauna and flora. In this century the list is not much longer. Paul Nash made numerous forays into book illustration as did his two distinguished students at the Royal College, Edward Bawden and Eric Ravilious. Apart from them the list of modern English painter-illustrators is barely more than could be counted on the fingers of two hands. John Nash was one of the few contemporary English painters who consistently carried out illustration commissions and without detriment to his painting.

The reason the Nashes, Bawden and Ravilious took so easily to media other than oil paint and a 20 in. $\times$ 30 in. canvas is that they are what I would call designer painters. As early as 1918 a critic, J. G. Fletcher wrote in *New Paths*:

'It is in landscape decoration, pure and simple, that he [Paul Nash] excels, as does his brother, John Nash. There is an oriental quality in much of their work.'[13] This so-called oriental quality is the result of a search for basic forms as opposed to an attempt at rendering the visual scene and the transitory effects of light on the landscape. Such design discipline can be applied in any medium.

John Nash never sought book illustrating commissions but when they came his way he welcomed them and he tackled them with skill and usually with pleasure, for the commissions he received were invariably for subjects that interested him – the countryside, flowers, fishing and other rural pursuits, and of course humour. He was never asked to illustrate *Hamlet* or *Wuthering Heights*, which was just as well. Such subjects were not for him. He always worked within his limitations and so was able to channel all his talents into the subject of his choice. His only concern was that this illustration work should not interfere with his painting.

In the autumn of 1976 Anthony d'Offay organised an exhibition of John Nash's wood engravings, illustrations and drawings of plants. For this John Nash wrote a little essay which d'Offay published under the title of *The Artist Plantsman*. It is a pleasant piece of autobiographical writing tracing his interest in flowers from the time when he was very young and used to visit his uncle's farm near Wallingford. He concludes his short discourse with these words:

'For nearly seventy years I have drawn plants for love or necessity and have never destroyed even slight sketches or notes in case they should be needed for reference (publishers can have an awkward habit of asking for illustrations in the "dead" season). In any case, I feel a slight pencil flourish even of part of a plant is more valuable than a photograph. The open innocent countenance of a Daisy or Anemone may seem easy to draw, but they too can prove to be a snare, and sometimes I prefer the hooded Labiates, helmetted Monkshood and Balsam, or the leering countenance of Foxglove and Pentstemon.'

No doubt some day, and it cannot be too soon, someone better qualified than I am will write a book about John Nash the painter. I think, as I near the end of this brief study, I know why so much should have been written about his brother Paul's work and so little about his. It is summed up in Sickert's often quoted remark:

'Paul with his head where a poet should be, in the clouds, and John like the child the painter should be, putting his brush in his mouth to tell us what he has seen in the field or on the farm that afternoon.'[14] The critics are at home with poets, theirs after all is a business of ideas and words, but to deal with someone who was just a painter, that's a different matter. John Nash is a painter's painter, and it will probably take an artist to write about that side of his work.

To have dealt with John Nash's graphic work is a much easier task. To decide what is the most important side of this illustrative work is more difficult. There are some who think his comic drawings surpass everything else he has done in illustration; others who reckon his wood engravings of plants and flowers to be the equal of anything done on wood in the years between the wars. There are yet others – and I count myself among these – who think his pen-drawn illustrations for *Seven Short Stories*, *Cobbett's Rural Rides*, *Men and the Fields* or for *Selborne*, which uniquely combine humour, botany and landscape into one felicitous whole, the best things he has done and worthy to rank with his 'serious work', his paintings and watercolour drawings.

John Nash may have regarded all this as a secondary part of his work, but there can be few graphic artists who would not gladly have settled for any one side of this work as their main contribution to the art of illustration.

NOTES

CHAPTER 1   1 *Poet and Painter*, being the correspondence between *Gordon Bottomley and Paul Nash 1910-1946*. Oxford 1955. Letter to Gordon Bottomley 12 July 1912.
2 Letter to John and Griselda Lewis 29 August 1951.
3 Letter to G.L. undated September 1956.
4 Letter to J.L. 25 October 1965.
5 Letter to G.L. 15 April 1963.
6 Letter to J.L. 22 November 1967.
7 Letter to J.L. 24 June 1968.
8 Letter to G.L. and J.L. undated January 1969.
9 Letter to J.L. undated September 1972.
10 Natalie Bevan (formerly Sieveking).
11 Letter to G.L. and J.L. 17 April 1973.
12 Letter to G.L. undated September 1956.

CHAPTER 2   1 *The Triumph of Caesar* is a set of nine frescoes painted between 1486 and 1494. Fry was given the job of restoring one of these frescoes, *The Picture Bearers.*
2 Roger Fry's *Retrospect*, first published in *Vision and Design* 1920.
3 *Paint and Prejudice*. C. R. W. Nevinson. Methuen 1937.
4 *Poet and Painter. op. cit.*
5 *The Artist Plantsman.* John Nash. Anthony d'Offay 1976.
6 Introduction by Frederick Gore A.R.A. to the Catalogue of John Nash's Retrospective Exhibition at the Royal Academy of Arts 1967.
7 Letter to G.L. and J.L. undated 1950.
8 *The Artist Plantsman. op. cit.*
9 Edwin Mullins in *The Sunday Telegraph* September 1967.
10 John Russell in *The Sunday Times* September 1967.
11 Maurice Wiggin in *The Sunday Times* March 1969.
12 Letter to Gordon Bottomley 13 July 1912.

CHAPTER 3   1 Sidney Schiff on John Nash in *British Artists of Today*. The Fleuron 1925.
2 *The London Mercury*. Vol. 1 No. 3. January 1920.
3 *Illustration*. Vol IV No. 5 *Notes on Artists*. Signed R.D.
4 *Confessions of an Incurable Collector*. Desmond Coke. Chapman & Hall 1928.
5 *A History of Wood Engraving*. D. P. Bliss. Dent 1928.
6 *The London Mercury*. Vol. 17 No. 109. November 1928.
7 *The Artist Plantsman. op. cit.*
8 *Alphabet & Image* 3. December 1946.
   The Twentieth Century Book. John Lewis. Studio Vista. 1967.
9 *The Golden Hind*. October 1922 and January 1923.
10 Letter to J.L. 8 November 1950.
11 *Times Literary Supplement*. 1 January 1954.
12 Letter to J.L. 3 September 1958.
13 *New Paths*. Verse, Prose and Pictures 1917-18. 'Tendencies in present-day English Art' by J. G. Fletcher.
14 In an article about the 1916 London Group show.

BIBLIOGRAPHY

Section A Books and Booklets illustrated wholly, or in part,
by John Nash

DRESSING GOWNS AND GLUE by Captain Lance de G. Sieveking DSC. With an
Introduction about the Verses by G. K. Chesterton and an Introduction about
the Drawings by Max Beerbohm and an Introduction about all concerned by
Cecil Palmer. Edited by Paul Nash. Cecil Palmer and Hayward 1919.
24.5 × 18.5 cms   pp (8) 9–47
Pictorial boards.
Frontispiece, title page vignette, 15 line drawings in text and illustrations on
covers.
*This book was published in September 1919. A second edition was issued in the same
month.*

THE SUN CALENDAR 1920 arranged by Paul Nash. With illustrations by Paul and
John Nash and Rupert Lee. Sun Engraving Company Ltd.
25 × 18.5 cms   pp 28
Includes six half-page line drawings and a woodcut on the inside back
wrapper by J.N.

THE NOUVEAU POOR A Romance of Real Life in West London after the Late
War by Belinda Blinders. Chapman and Hall 1921.
18.5 × 12 cms   pp (19) 2–165
Brown cloth.
Frontispiece and 15 full-page line drawings and cover design.
*'Belinda Blinders' was the pseudonym of Desmond Coke, a friend of John Nash and
collector of his work.*

DIRECTIONS TO SERVANTS by the Rev. Jonathan Swift DD. The Golden
Cockerel Press 1925.
25.5 × 19 cms   pp (8) 1–35
Green marbled boards vellum backed, title gold blocked on spine, uncut.
10 wood engravings in text, wood engraved vignette on title page and for tailpiece.
Edition limited to 380 (numbered) copies of which Nos. 1–30 were bound in
full vellum and signed by the artist.

OVID'S ELEGIES translated by Christopher Marlowe together with THE EPIGRAMS
OF SIR JOHN DAVIES. Etchells and Macdonald 1925.
23 × 14.5 cms   pp (6) 1–102
Buckram backed paper covered boards decorated on front, uncut.
Frontispiece and six full-page wood engravings, wood engraved vignettes on
title page and for tail piece.
Edition limited to 625 numbered copies. 35 additional copies were printed on
hand-made paper, numbered I–XXXV and signed by the artist.

123

BATS IN THE BELFRY The Collected Nonsense Poems of L. de Giberne Sieveking with Introductions by G. K. Chesterton and Max Beerbohm. Routledge 1926.
25 × 15.25 cms   pp (17) 1–115
Green cloth gilt, gold blocked decorations on front and spine.
48 line drawings of which 16 appear full-page, 4 half-tones, cover design.
50 special copies, bound in quarter blue calf, spine blocked in gold with blue cloth sides, were printed, and signed by the author and the artist.
The two introductions and 21 of the illustrations first appeared in 'Dressing Gowns and Glue'.

CATALOGUE OF ALPINE AND HERBACEOUS PLANTS. Six Hills Nursery 1926.
22.5 × 15.5 cms   pp (4) 1–96
Buckram backed paper covered boards decorated on front.
7 full page and 2 half page hand-coloured line drawings.
This special edition limited to 100 numbered copies signed by the artist.

POISONOUS PLANTS Deadly Dangerous and Suspect. Engraved on wood and with an Introduction by John Nash with Brief Descriptions by W. Dallimore. Edited by Dr. A. W. Hill, FRS. Etchells and Macdonald 1927.
50.25 × 18.5 cms   pp (12) 3–85
Silk cloth, sides backed in green cloth, front blocked in gold with plant design, uncut.
20 full-page wood engravings, wood engraved head piece and tail piece for contents pages, cover design.
Edition limited to 250 numbered copies, printed by the Curwen Press on Renker's Ingres paper.

THE BOOK OF THE TREE edited by Georgina Mase. Peter Davies 1927.
20.5 × 12.5 cms   pp (44) 1–239
Green cloth, gold blocked title on spine.
Wood engraved frontispiece only, repeated on d.w.

THE EARLY WHISTLER by Wilfrid Gibson. Number 6 of the Ariel poems. Faber and Gwyer n.d. (1927).
18.5 × 12 cms   pp 4   Red wrappers.
Line drawing on front and one full-page illustration in colour line.
There was also an edition limited to 350 (unnumbered) copies on Zanders hand-made paper bound in white boards.

THE HOUSE IN THE COUNTRY by Bernadette Murphy. Putnam 1927.
19 × 11 cms   pp (8) 9–170
Wood engraved frontispiece on India paper only, repeated on d.w.

JIPPING STREET by Kathleen Woodward. Longmans Green 1928.
19.5 × 13.5 cms   pp (14) 3–157   Red cloth, paper label on spine.
Wood engraved frontispiece only, repeated on dust wrapper.

THE APOCRYPHA according to the Authorised Version. Cresset Press 1929.
32.5 × 20.75 cms   pp (10) 1–406
Vellum, black leather label blocked in gold on spine.
Includes one full-page wood engraving by John Nash of the murder of Holofernes.
Edition limited to 450 copies on mould-made paper.

THE ANATOMY OF DESSERT by E. A. Bunyard. Dulau 1929.
20.5×14 cms   pp (7) 1–134
Green buckram, title gold blocked on spine.
Wood engraved frontispiece only printed in green, repeated in red on d.w.
Edition limited to 1,000 copies signed by the author.

CELESTE and other sketches by Stephen Hudson. The Blackamore Press 1930.
20.5×13.5 cms   pp (12) 13–101
Green silk cloth, gold blocked on front and spine. Six full-page wood
engravings.
Edition limited to 700 copies of which 50, signed by author and artist, were
printed on Japanese vellum.
'Stephen Hudson' was the pseudonym of Sidney Schiff, a friend of John Nash and
collector of his work.

THE NEW FLORA AND SILVA Edited by E. H. M. Cox FLS. Vols 2 and 3.
Dulau 1930 and 1931.
24.5×14.25 cms   Vol 2 pp (4) 1–295   Vol. 3 pp (4) 1–296
Blue buckram, gold blocked title on spine. Vol. 2 four full-page line drawings
of plants; Vol. 3 four coloured plates after watercolours.
'The New Flora and Silva' was a quarterly magazine that was reissued in hard covers.

THE SHEPHEARDS CALENDER by Edmund Spenser. The Cresset Press 1930.
32.25×19.25 cms   pp (23) 2–133
Silk cloth sides backed in parchment, gold blocked title on spine, uncut.
Frontispiece and 12 head pieces coloured by the stencil process.
Edition limited to 350 copies on hand-made paper and three copies on Roman
vellum of which number one was accompanied by the original illustrations.

RURAL RIDES by William Cobbett edited with an introduction by G. D. H. and
Margaret Cole and a map of Cobbett's country by A. E. Taylor. Three vols.
Peter Davies 1930.
25×15.25 cms   pp (56) 2–1064
Marbled boards backed with cloth, gold blocked titles on spines.
33 line drawings for tail pieces, three being repeated as vignettes on the title
pages.
Edition limited to one thousand sets of three volumes.

WHEN THOU WAST NAKED a story by T. F. Powys. Golden Cockerel Press 1931.
23.5×15 cms   pp (8) 1–65
Pattern paper boards backed in blue morocco, t.e.g., uncut.
Three wood engravings in text, another on title page and another as tail piece.
Edition limited to 500 numbered copies.

SEVEN SHORT STORIES by Walter de la Mare. Faber and Faber 1931.
22.5×15 cms   pp (12) 13–195
Red cloth, gold blocked on front and spine.
Eight full-page line drawings coloured by the stencil process, uncoloured
vignette on title page and end page, the latter repeated on d.w.
Also issued in a limited edition of 170 numbered copies, each signed by the
author and artist, printed on Italian hand-made paper and bound in vellum.

ONE HUNDRED AND ONE BALLADES (contributed by 18 poets). Cobden Sanderson 1931.
21.25 × 13.25 cms   pp (12) 1–108
Yellow cloth, gold blocked on spine.
20 line drawings of which 17 are full-page, one repeated on d.w.
The book was published in October 1931. A second edition was issued in December.

THE CURIOUS GARDENER by Jason Hill. Faber and Faber 1932.
22.5 × 13.5 cms   pp (4) 5–173
Brown cloth, gold blocked on spine.
Five full-page line drawings, another on title page and another as tail piece to the preface, one illustration repeated on d.w.
'Jason Hill' was the pseudonym of Dr. Anthony Hampton.

RHYMES FOR EVERYMAN by Ernest Rhys. Lovat Dickson 1933.
18.5 × 12 cms   pp (7) 8–64
Green cloth, gold blocked on spine.
Line drawn frontispiece and tailpiece only.

FLOWERS AND FACES by H. E. Bates. Golden Cockerel Press 1935.
25 × 18 cms   pp (8) 5–52
Marbled cloth backed in green morocco, t.e.g., uncut.
Four full-page wood engravings and wood engraved decorations on title page.
Edition limited to 325 copies signed by the author, of which Nos. 1–6 were printed on vellum and 7–325 on Batchelor Hand-made Paper.

BUCKS SHELL GUIDE by John Nash with notes on monuments by Katherine A. Esdaile. Batsford (1937).
22.5 × 17.5 cms   pp (4) 1–45
Glazed card wrappers, ring backed, photos on both sides.
Beech leaf design on fly leaves, four flower drawings in text and reproduction of two paintings.
This booklet was reissued by Faber in 1939.

WILD FLOWERS IN BRITAIN by Robert Gathorne-Hardy. Batsford 1938.
21.75 × 13.25 cms   pp (8) 1–120
Green cloth.
Includes frontispiece and three plates lithographed in colour, 24 line drawings in text, four coloured litho design on d.w.

PLANTS WITH PERSONALITIES by Patrick M. Synge. Lindsay Drummond, 6-7 Buckingham St., WC2, n.d.
22.5 × 14 cms   pp (16) 17-243
Green cloth, gold blocked on spine.
Includes eight full-page flower drawings.
There was a cheaper edition on thinner paper, in a slightly smaller format, n.d., issued by the same publishers from 2 Guilford Place, London WC1.

MEN AND THE FIELDS by Adrian Bell. Batsford 1939.
21 × 13.75 cms   pp (4) 2–155
Brown cloth, gold blocked on spine.
Frontispiece and five plates lithographed in colour, 30 line drawings in text, coloured litho designs on d.w.

THE CONTEMPLATIVE GARDENER by Jason Hill. Faber and Faber 1940.
21.75 × 13 cms   pp (6) 7–214
Blue cloth, gold blocked on spine.
22 full-page line drawings of flowers, one repeated on d.w.

ALMANACK OF HOPE by John Pudney. John Lane 1944.
16 × 13.25 cms   pp (8) 9–30
Decorated boards.
12 full-page line drawings, decorated title page and end page, title page design
repeated on cover and d.w.
Also issued in a special edition of 50 numbered copies, signed by the author,
printed on mould-made paper and bound in red cloth.

A PROSPECT OF FLOWERS by Andrew Young. Cape 1945.
20 × 13 cms   pp (4) 5–194
Green cloth, gold blocked on spine.
Line drawn frontispiece and d.w. design only.

FIVE GRAVES AT NIJMEGEN by Eric Baume. Batsford 1945.
21.75 × 14 cms   pp (2) 3–31
Pink pictorial wrapper.
Line drawn cover design and colophon only.

A HANDBOOK OF PRINTING TYPES by John Lewis. W. S. Cowell Ltd, distributed
by Faber and Faber, 1947.
21.5 × 14 cms   pp 96
Cloth covers printed with Speede's map of Suffolk.
Includes two half-page line and colour drawings.

ENGLISH GARDEN FLOWERS by John Nash. Duckworth 1948.
28 × 21.25 cms   pp (7) 8–130
Quarter bound in red paper-covered boards decorated on front.
12 plates lithographed in colour and cover design.

THE NATURAL HISTORY OF SELBORNE by Gilbert White. Lutterworth Press 1951.
19.5 × 12.75 cms   pp (10) 11–308
Green cloth, gold blocked on spine.
Frontispiece and 11 full-page line drawings, 19 line drawings in text,
frontispiece elaborated on d.w.

PARNASSIAN MOLEHILL an anthology of Suffolk verse edited by the Earl of
Cranbrook. W. S. Cowell Ltd, Ipswich 1953.
20.75 × 16.25 cms   pp (16) 5–264
White cloth decorated with a repeat pattern of a wild rose vignette printed in
four colours, slip case.
Frontispiece, decorated title page and half-title, 46 line drawings in text.
Edition limited to 500 numbered copies on Basingwerk parchment.

THE NINTH ALDEBURGH FESTIVAL PROGRAMME BOOK 15–24 June 1956.
24.5 × 18 cms   pp 86
Grey decorated wrappers.
Six line drawings in text, vignette on title page and cover design.

127

THE TRANQUIL GARDENER by Robert Gathorne-Hardy. Nelson 1958.
22.5 × 15.5 cms   pp (12) 1–201
Green cloth, gold blocked on spine.
Frontispiece and three plates in colour, 28 line drawings, coloured floral design on d.w.

BENHAM'S CALENDAR FOR 1958 captions by Ronald Blythe. Benham and Co Ltd, Colchester.
21.25 × 31.25 cms   pp 12
Green paper wrappers.
12 half-page drawings in colour line.

HAPPY NEW LEAR Designed for Guinness by S. H. Benson Ltd (1959).
23 × 16 cms   pp 12
Pictorial wrappers in four colours.
Numerous comic drawings in colour line.

THORNTREE MEADOWS by Roger Nett. Nelson, 1st English ed. 1960.
22 × 13.5 cms   pp (6) 1–138
Line drawn frontispiece and seven line drawings in text, eight plates in colour line.

THE NATIVE GARDEN by Robert Gathorne-Hardy. Nelson 1961.
22.5 × 15.25 cms   pp (12) 1-175
Green cloth, gold blocked on spine.
Frontispiece and five plates in colour, 30 line drawings in text, coloured floral design on d.w.

THE BBC BOOK OF THE COUNTRYSIDE edited by Arthur Phillips. BBC 1963.
22.75 × 14.5 cms   pp (4) 5–153
Beige cloth, gold blocked on front and spine.
Includes six full-page line drawings.

THE ART OF ANGLING by Trevor Housby. Evans Brothers Ltd. 1965.
21 × 13.5 cms   pp (5) 6–199
Grey tweed cloth.   Includes eight line drawings.

FLOWER DRAWINGS BY JOHN NASH Warren Editions 1969.
50 × 37.5 cms
12 reproductions of flower drawings, printed on hand-made paper, unbound in lavender paper portfolio with canvas spine.
Limited to 65 copies, each sheet numbered and signed by the artist.
11 of the 12 drawings first appeared, in a greatly reduced size, in 'Plants with Personalities', 'The Tranquil Gardener' and 'The Native Garden'.

WICKEN SEDGE FEN by F. J. Bingley and S. M. Walters. The National Trust. 1966.
21.5 × 13.7 cms   pp 8
Suede pictorial wrapper with line drawn cover design.
26 line drawings in the text.

THE NATURAL HISTORY OF SELBORNE by Gilbert White, introduction by the Earl of Cranbrook. The Limited Editions Club 1972.
29.75 × 21 cms   pp (4) 5–275

Quarter bound in calf, decorated paper covered boards, gold blocked on spine;
slipcase as boards.
16 full-page illustrations lithographed in colour, 15 line drawings in text and
vignette on title page.

Section B Dust wrappers and cover designs by John Nash excluding those for books listed in Section A

CATALOGUES OF SIX HILLS NURSERY, STEVENAGE, HERTS. Many between 1925 and
1936/7. Plant drawings for covers, decorations on title pages.

VEGETABLES FOR EPICURES George Bunyard and Co Ltd, Maidstone c. 1925.
Line drawing for front of wrapper.

BBC HOUSEHOLD TALKS 1928. BBC 1929.
Line drawing printed in three colours for front of d.w.

THE BEST OF ENGLAND by H. A. Vachell. Hodder and Stoughton 1933.
Line drawings for front of d.w.

OPEN THE CAGE by Sybil Fountain. Howe (1934).
Line drawing for front of d.w.

THE BALCONY by Adrian Bell. Cobden Sanderson 1934.
Drawing in three colours for front of d.w.

YOUNG PASQUIER by Georges Duhamel. Dent 1935.
Drawing in three colours for front of d.w.

GENTIANS by David Wilkie. Country Life 1936.
Lithograph in two colours for front of d.w.

IRIS CULTURE FOR AMATEURS by L. F. Pesel and R. E. S. Spender. Country Life
1937.
Lithographic d.w. drawn direct on to the stone and printed in three colours.

SOME FLOWERS by V. Sackville West. Cobden Sanderson 1937.
Design of flowers in three colour litho for upper cover.

THE CURWEN PRESS NEWSLETTER No. 14 November 1937.
Autolithograph in four colours for front of wrapper.

WILD BIRDS IN BRITAIN by Seton Gordon. Batsford 1938.
Colour lithographs for front and back of d.w.

WILD ANIMALS IN BRITAIN by Frances Pitt. Batsford 1938.
Colour lithographs for front and back of d w.

BEAUTIFUL BRITAIN Country Life Calendar 1940.
Autolithograph in three colours for cover.

BRITISH BIRDS IN THEIR HAUNTS by Rev. C. A. Johns. Routledge 1948.
Colour lithograph for front of d.w.

BRITISH BUTTERFLIES AND MOTHS by Dr. W. E. Kirby. Routledge 1949.
Colour lithograph for front of d.w.

BRITISH TREES AND SHRUBS by Rev. C. A. Johns. Routledge 1949.
Colour lithograph for front of d.w.

FLOWERS OF THE FIELD by Rev. C. A. Johns. Routledge 1949.
Colour lithograph for front of d.w.

OUTLINE an autobiography by Paul Nash. Faber 1949.
Line drawing for front of d.w.

S. H. BENSON LTD SIXTIETH ANNIVERSARY LUNCHEON MENU 2nd October 1953.
Decorations in colour line for front and back of wrappers from designs for a
commemorative tankard.

VEGETABLE OILS AND FATS Unilever 1955.
Reproduction of a watercolour for front of wrapper.

THE WORLD OF NATURE BBC 1959.
Reproduction of a watercolour painted for this pamphlet.

BY THE WAY an occasional bulletin from the Curwen Press. Autumn 1959.
Line drawing of flower for front of wrapper.

FIELD STUDIES COUNCIL, FLATFORD MILL CENTRE 1960.
Line drawing for front cover of a leaflet presented to HRH the Duke of
Edinburgh on the occasion of his visit July 8th 1960.

SHELL MEX AND BP SHILLING GUIDE TO DORSET 1963.
Cover design in full colour for front and back wrapper reproduced from the
Shell Country Guide series of advertisements.

SHELL MEX AND BP SHILLING GUIDE TO CAMBRIDGESHIRE AND HUNTINGDONSHIRE
1964.
Cover design in full colour for front and back wrapper.

Section C Some Periodicals and Annuals containing illustrations by John Nash

NEW PATHS Verse, Prose, Pictures 1917–1918. C. W. Beaumont.
Reproduction of the watercolour 'An Italian Garden'.

ART AND LETTERS
Spring 1919. One full-page comic drawing.
Summer 1919. One full-page landscape, line drawing.
Autumn 1919. One full-page comic drawing.

LAND AND WATER
Weekly issues June and July 1919. Numerous comic drawings illustrating
theatre reviews.

NEW WITNESS
1st August 1919. Line drawings.

ILLUSTRATION Sun Engraving Co.
Vol. IV No. 5 1919. Reproductions.

THE MONTHLY CHAPBOOK Poetry Bookshop.
No. 3, September 1919. One full-page line drawing.
No. 38, June 1923. Two full-page woodcuts.

(No. 39), The Chapbook 1924. One woodcut.
No. 40, The Chapbook 1925. One wood engraving.

THE OWL
No. 2, October 1919. One full-page comic drawing.

MODERN ART 1919 SERIES Colour Magazine.
Reproduction in colour of 'A Gloucestershire Landscape'.

THE APPLE
First Quarter, January 1920. One full-page comic drawing.

THE GOLDEN HIND
No. 1, October 1922. One full-page lithograph.
No. 2, January 1923. One full-page lithograph.

THE LONDON MERCURY
January 1923, No. 39. Wood engraving 'Sheep Shearing'.
February 1928, No. 100. Two reproductions of wood engravings from
Poisonous Plants.
October 1929, No. 120. Reproduction of wood engraved frontispiece to *The
Anatomy of Dessert*.
February 1931, No. 136. Portrait of John Nash by Powys Evans.

MASTERPIECES OF MODERN ART Colour Magazine.
January 1926. Reproduction in colour of 'The Thatched Cottage'.

THE WOODCUT
Vol. 1, 1927. Reproduction of a wood engraving from *Poisonous Plants*.

THE LISTENER
1933 and 1934. Many plant drawings illustrating articles.

SIGNATURE
No. 12, July 1939. Autolithograph in four colours, used as an advertisement for
the Baynard Press.

THE COUNTRYMAN
Vol. 43, No. 2, Summer 1951. One comic line drawing.
Vol. 56, No. 2, Summer 1959. Pen drawing on cover.

THE SATURDAY BOOK
No. 7, 1947. Five line drawings illustrating an article.
No. 13, 1953. Three line drawings in two colours illustrating a poem.
No. 17, 1957. Six line drawings for 'Cottage Window Plants' drawn and
described by John Nash RA.

FAR AND WIDE Guest Keen and Nettlefold.
No. 49, 1959. Two line and colour illustrations to an article.

LAND Shell Chemical Company.
No. 10, Winter 1960/61. One watercolour and three drawings illustrating an
article.
No. 12, Spring 1962. Three comic drawings illustrating an article.

GARDENERS CHRONICLE AND NEW HORTICULTURALIST
March 21st 1969. Reproduction of two wood engravings from *Poisonous Plants*
in 'Clarence Elliott VMH a personal memoir by John Nash'.

WORDS ETCETERA
Vol. 1, No. 1, 1971. Cover design and line drawn illustration to a poem.

Section D A Miscellany

THE POETRY BOOKSHOP BROADSIDES *c.* 1921.
No. 5, 'Windy Nights' by R. L. Stevenson. Colour line.
No. 8, 'The Beasts' by Walt Whitman. Colour line.
No. 11, 'Sister Awake'. Colour line.

THE POETRY BOOKSHOP RHYME SHEETS *c.* 1923.
No. 3, 'On a certain lady at court' by Alexander Pope. Colour line.
No. 5, 'A Memory' by William Allingham. Colour line.
No. 14, 'To a Butterfly' by William Wordsworth. Colour line.
No. 18, 'Leisure' by W. H. Davies. Colour line.

THE POETRY BOOKSHOP: THE NEW BROADSIDES *c.* 1923.
No. 8, 'Song of Myself' by Walt Whitman. Colour line.

PRESS ADVERTISEMENT FOR DUNLOP *c.* 1925.
Comic drawings.

PRESS ADVERTISEMENT FOR EMPIRE MARKETING BOARD 1929.
Wood engraving of Southern Rhodesia Tobacco (reproduced in the Curwen Press Specimen Book of Newspaper Settings and in Posters and Publicity 1929, "Commercial Art" Annual published by the Studio).

THE COUNTRYMAN'S ENGLAND by Dorothy Hartley. Batsford 1935.
Reproduction of the painting 'Threshing' for frontispiece.

LEAFLET FOR JOHN DICKINSON'S 'EVENSYDE' PRINTING PAPER 1935.
Reproduction of the wood engraving 'Black Bryony' from *Poisonous Plants*.

COUNTRY LIFE CALENDAR 1949.
Reproduction of a watercolour.

PRESS ADVERTISEMENT FOR CRITALL WINDOWS *c.* 1952.
Line drawing.

POST OFFICE POSTER *c.* 1965.
Reproduction of a watercolour.

PERSONAL CHRISTMAS CARDS, mainly post-war and for most years up to 1970.
Line and colour line.

Section E Some references to John Nash's Graphic Work

THE PRINT COLLECTOR'S QUARTERLY, October 1921.
'The Modern Woodcut' Part 2 by Herbert Furst. One illustration.

CONTEMPORARY ENGLISH WOODCUTS by Campbell Dodgson, CBE. Duckworth 1922. Limited to 550 copies.
Two illustrations.

ARTWORK
No. 2, October 1924. Reproduction of wood engraving 'Pigs'.
No. 9, March-May 1927. Reproduction of wood engraving 'The Birds Paradise'.

BRITISH ARTISTS OF TODAY, NO. 2 JOHN NASH The Fleuron 1925.
Two page introduction by Sidney Schiff and 17 half-tone reproductions of watercolours and oil paintings.

DEUTSCHE NORDMARK 1926.
'Eine Englische Maler John Nash'.

DRAWING AND DESIGN Vol. 1, No. 1, July 1926.
'Modern English Wood Engraving' by W. Gaunt.   Three illustrations.

THE HISTORY OF WOOD ENGRAVING by D. P. Bliss. Dent 1928.
Two illustrations.

FRANCIS UNWIN, ETCHER AND DRAUGHTSMAN ed. John Nash. The Fleuron 1928.

THE WOODCUT Vol. 3, 1929.
'The Wood Engravings of John Nash' by W. A. Thorpe.
12pp with four illustrations.
The de luxe edition of this volume, limited to 80 copies on hand-made paper,
had as the frontispiece a wood engraving 'The Two Tugs', signed by John Nash.

THIRTY YEARS OF BRITISH ART by Sir Joseph Duveen Bt.
The Studio 1930.   Two illustrations.

THE STUDIO
March 1930. 'British wood engraving of the present day' by Maximilien Vox.
One illustration.
May 1931. 'John Nash' by Frank Rutter.
12pp with 12 illustrations.
February 1939. 'Wood engraving of today' by Gwendolen Raverat.
One illustration.
May 1939. 'New watercolours by John Nash' by E. N. Wright.
2pp with four illustrations.

MODERN BOOK ILLUSTRATION IN GREAT BRITAIN AND AMERICA The Studio 1931.
Two illustrations.

WOOD ENGRAVING AND WOODCUTS by Clare Leighton. The Studio 1932.
One illustration.

PICTURE POST April 1st 1939.
'John Nash' by Dr. John Rothenstein in Great British Masters Series No. 27.
4pp with three coloured reproductions of paintings, and six other illustrations.

THE ARTIST January 1945.
'John Nash' by Richard Seddon in the series 'Artists of Note'. Three illustrations.

ALPHABET AND IMAGE No. 3, December 1946.
'The Engravings and Book Decorations of John Nash' by Frances Sarzano.
17pp with 28 illustrations.

THE ART BULLETIN No. 24, Spring 1948. Published by the Fine Art Trade Guild.
'A Master of English Landscape: John Nash, ARA' by Robert Bevan.
Four illustrations.

OUTLINE an autobiography by Paul Nash. Faber 1949.

IMAGE No. 5, Autumn 1950.
'English Wood Engraving 1900-1950' by Thomas Balston.
Four illustrations.

ARK No. 1, October 1950. The Magazine of the Royal College of Art.
'Book Illustration' by John Nash.   Two illustrations.

PAUL NASH by Anthony Bertram. Faber 1955.

POET AND PAINTER The correspondence between Gordon Bottomley and Paul Nash 1910-1946. Oxford 1955.

MODERN ENGLISH PAINTERS 2: LEWIS TO MOORE by Sir John Rothenstein. Eyre and Spottiswoode 1956.
Essay of 12pp with two illustrations of paintings.

JOHN NASH CBE RA Catalogue of the exhibition of Paintings and drawings by John Nash at the Royal Academy of Arts 1967.
11pp introduction by Frederick Gore, cover illustration and two portrait photographs.

COUNTRY LIFE. 7 September 1967. 'John Nash's Home-Grown Vision' by Christopher Neve. Five illustrations.

ILLUSTRATED LONDON NEWS. 9 September 1967. 'In Praise of the English Countryside' by Andrew Causey. Five illustrations.

JOHN NASH Catalogue of the Exhibition at The Minories, Colchester 1967.
3pp introduction by John Lewis, five illustrations.

THE COUNTRYMAN Vol. 69, Autumn 1967.
'John Nash RA' by Ronald Blythe. 10pp with five illustrations.

THE TWENTIETH CENTURY BOOK by John Lewis. Studio Vista 1967.
Three illustrations.

ILLUSTRATED BRISTOL NEWS. April 1975. 'John Nash in Bristol' by John Sampson. One illustration.

EAST ANGLIAN MAGAZINE. June 1975. 'John Nash, RA. Father of Essex Landscape' by Ray Rushton. Four illustrations.

THE SUNDAY TIMES Colour Supplement, 31 August 1975. 'The Sense of Place' by William Feaver. 6pp with eight coloured illustrations and coloured photograph of the artist.

THE ARTIST PLANTSMAN by John Nash. Anthony d'Offay 1976.
7pp of text and two line drawings. Limited to 450 copies.
The text of this article was reprinted in *The Garden*, Journal of the Royal Horticultural Society Vol. 102 Part 3 March 1977. A water colour by John Nash of *Eomecon chionantha* was reproduced in colour on the front cover.

ARTISTS AT CURWEN by Pat Gilmour. Tate Gallery 1977.
One coloured illustration.

This book has been designed by John Lewis and
printed on Basingwerk Parchment by The Compton
Press in collaboration with Skelton's Press.
It is set in 12/15 point Monotype Baskerville and
bound by Weatherby-Woolnough Limited.